BARRON

RALPI

Invisible Man

BY

Anthony S. Abbott
Professor of English
Davidson College

SERIES COORDINATOR

Murray Bromberg
Principal, Wang High School of Queens
Holliswood, New York

Past President
High School Principals Association of New York City

BARRON'S EDUCATIONAL SERIES, INC.

ACKNOWLEDGMENTS

Our thanks to Milton Katz and Julius Liebb for their advisory
assistance on the *Book Notes* series.

All inquiries should be addressed to:
Barron's Educational Series, Inc.
250 Wireless Blvd.
Hauppauge, NY 11788

Library of Congress Catalog Card No. 85-3938

International Standard Book No. 0-8120-3520-8

Library of Congress Cataloging in Publication Data

Abbott, Anthony S.
   Ralph Ellison's Invisible man.

   (Barron's book notes)
   Bibliography: p. 127.
   Summary: A guide to reading "Invisible Man" with a
critical and appreciative mind encouraging analysis of
plot, style, form, and structure. Also includes background
on the author's life and times, sample tests, term paper
suggestions, and a reading list.
   1. Ellison, Ralph. Invisible man. [1. Ellison,
Ralph. Invisible man. 2. American literature—History
and criticism] I. Title. II. Series.
PS3555.L6251532 1985   813'.54   85-3938
ISBN 0-8120-3520-8 (pbk.)

CONTENTS

ADVISORY BOARD

HOW TO USE THIS BOOK

You have to know how to approach literature in order to get the most out of it. This *Barron's Book Notes* volume follows a plan based on methods used by some of the best students to read a work of literature.

Begin with the guide's section on the author's life and times. As you read, try to form a clear picture of the author's personality, circumstances, and motives for writing the work. This background usually will make it easier for you to hear the author's tone of voice, and follow where the author is heading.

Then go over the rest of the introductory material—such sections as those on the plot, characters, setting, themes, and style of the work. Underline, or write down in your notebook, particular things to watch for, such as contrasts between characters and repeated literary devices. At this point, you may want to develop a system of symbols to use in marking your text as you read. (Of course, you should only mark up a book you own, not one that belongs to another person or a school.) Perhaps you will want to use a different letter for each character's name, a different number for each major theme of the book, a different color for each important symbol or literary device. Be prepared to mark up the pages of your book as you read. Put your marks in the margins so you can find them again easily.

Now comes the moment you've been waiting for—the time to start reading the work of literature. You may want to put aside your *Barron's Book Notes* volume until you've read the work all the way through. Or you may want to alternate, reading the *Book Notes* analysis of each section as soon as you have finished reading the corresponding part of the original. Before you move on, reread crucial passages you don't fully understand. (Don't take this guide's analysis for granted—make up your own mind as to what the work means.)

Once you've finished the whole work of literature, you may want to review it right away, so you can firm up your ideas about what it means. You may want to leaf through the book concentrating on passages you marked in reference to one character or one theme. This is also a good time to reread the *Book Notes* introductory material, which pulls together insights on specific topics.

When it comes time to prepare for a test or to write a paper, you'll already have formed ideas about the work. You'll be able to go back through it, refreshing your memory as to the author's exact words and perspective, so that you can support your opinions with evidence drawn straight from the work. Patterns will emerge, and ideas will fall into place; your essay question or term paper will almost write itself. Give yourself a dry run with one of the sample tests in the guide. These tests present both multiple-choice and essay questions. An accompanying section gives answers to the multiple-choice questions as well as suggestions for writing the essays. If you have to select a term paper topic, you may choose one from the list of suggestions in this book. This guide also provides you with a reading list, to help you when you start research for a term paper, and a selection of provocative comments by critics, to spark your thinking before you write.

THE AUTHOR
AND HIS TIMES

In 1952 a first novel by a virtually unknown black American named Ralph Waldo Ellison was published. Reviews of the novel were ecstatic, and in 1953 Ellison's *Invisible Man* won a prestigious National Book Award for Fiction. Suddenly the author was in great demand for interviews and lectures, and he found himself being compared not only with black writers like Richard Wright, but also with Herman Melville and Mark Twain, Ernest Hemingway and William Faulkner. *Invisible Man* was a phenomenon. In 1965 the phenomenon took on even greater proportions when a group of some 200 authors, critics, and editors named *Invisible Man* the most distinguished American novel of the previous twenty years.

The passage of time from 1965 to the mid-1980s did little to change the high regard for this remarkable novel. If a similar vote were taken in the mid-1980s, *Invisible Man* would likely be near the top of any list of the best American novels written since the end of World War II in 1945.

Who was the man who wrote this novel? What were his roots, his influences? What was his preparation for writing a book that has had such impact?

He was born on March 1, 1914, in Oklahoma City, the son of Lewis Ellison from Abbeyville, South Carolina and Ida Milsap Ellison from White Oak, Georgia. They had left the South and moved to Oklahoma to avoid the persecution of blacks, and to find the freedom of the frontier. Times were hard and the Ellisons were poor, but they were proud and ambitious for their children. Lewis Ellison, always a great reader, named his son for Ralph Waldo Emerson, the influential nineteenth century apostle of equality, self-reliance, and individualism. The son would eventually live up to his name. Ida Ellison brought back books, magazines, and newspapers from the white homes where she worked. She was a woman who spent her life fighting against economic and social injustice. "When I was in college," Ellison said, "my mother broke a segregated-housing ordinance in Oklahoma City, and they were throwing her in jail, and the NAACP would get her out. . . . She had that kind of forthrightness, and I like to think that that was much more valuable than anything literary that she gave me."

As Ralph Ellison grew up, he assimilated the liberal social and political ideals of his parents, but his first love was music. In high school he learned music theory and mastered the trumpet. There was much music in Oklahoma City, but especially there was jazz. Ellison heard the major jazz musicians of the age and became friends with a number of them. In 1933, when he entered Tuskegee Institute in Alabama as a scholarship student, he could already play and write both jazz and classical music and had also been involved with traditional black church music. It was a heritage that would have important influence on his writing.

Tuskegee Institute was Ellison's home for three years, and it is clearly the model for the college in *Invisible Man*. Not only do the buildings and environment in the novel strongly resemble Tuskegee, but the portrait of the Founder bears striking resemblance to the image of Tuskegee's founder, Booker T. Washington, about whom Ellison was clearly ambivalent. (For further analysis of the relationship between the Founder and Washington, read the discussion of Chapter 5 in The Story section.)

The conservative southern environment of Tuskegee was a shock to Ellison, but his intellectual development during his years at the college more than made up for the social disadvantages. The music faculty was excellent, as was the English department. He read the major works of the Harlem Renaissance, a sudden outburst of creativity by black writers that had begun in the 1920s, and dreamed of being a part of that movement himself. But the writer who excited him most was the famous poet T. S. Eliot. Ellison was stunned by the freshness and originality of Eliot's *The Waste Land*. "I was intrigued by its power to move me while eluding my understanding," he said later; and themes, symbols, images, and jazz rhythms of Eliot's great poem can be found in *Invisible Man*.

At the end of his junior year at Tuskegee, Ellison boarded a train and headed north to New York. He didn't have enough money to pay for his senior year at college and so set out for the place where gifted young blacks went to begin their careers—Harlem. Harlem meant black culture. It meant such jazz musicians as Duke Ellington and Teddy Wilson. It meant the Apollo Theater and the Savoy Ballroom, the Lafayette Theater and WPA Negro Theater Company. It meant a reunion with Ellison's old friend from Oklahoma City, the blues singer Jimmy Rushing; and it meant a new friendship with a leading poet of the Harlem Renaissance, Langston Hughes.

It also meant poverty and loneliness and a struggle to stay alive. Finally, and most important, it meant becoming friends with the most significant influence on his early writing, the novelist Richard Wright. Wright's collection of four stories, *Uncle Tom's Children* (1938), and his novel, *Native Son* (1940), made him the best known black writer in the United States during Ellison's period of apprenticeship in New York. In many ways, Wright was Ellison's first mentor. An active member of the U.S. Communist Party, Wright encouraged Ellison to write from a leftist point of view, because he believed at the time that the Communists had the best interests of blacks at heart. Under the influence of Wright and other Marxist thinkers, Ellison wrote more than twenty book reviews from 1937 to 1944 for a variety of leftist periodicals, especially *New Masses*. He praised writers dealing with social issues, such as Wright and John Steinbeck, and attacked writers who failed to give adequate attention to blacks' social, economic, and political problems.

But Ellison was never a Communist party member, and he never believed in communism. The limits that the party placed on individual expression were far too strong for him. As early as 1937, when he traveled to Dayton, Ohio, for his mother's funeral, Ellison had begun seeing himself as part of a larger literary tradition. He read not only writers of the Harlem Renaissance but also Ernest Hemingway, James Joyce, Gertrude Stein, and Fyodor Dostoevsky. Dostoevsky's *Notes from Underground* became one of the models for *Invisible Man*.

Ellison's preference for literature over politics led him to question the Communist party, and the Communist attitude toward blacks during World

War II caused a final rupture between the party in the United States and most of the black writers who had supported it during the 1930s. The Brotherhood section of *Invisible Man* strongly echoes the feelings of Ellison and other black writers that the party had been using blacks for its own ends.

In 1943, during World War II, Ellison joined the U.S. Merchant Marine because he wanted to make a contribution to the war effort in a service that was not segregated by race. He served for two years, and during that time he began to write fiction in earnest. Among his writings of the time were two of his best short stories, "Flying Home" and "King of the Bingo Game," both published in 1944. In these stories Ellison began to find a voice and an identity as a writer, and it is no accident that in the next year he started to write *Invisible Man*.

The novel, which began with the words "I am an invisible man" scribbled on a piece of paper in a friend's house in Vermont, took seven years to complete.

In writing *Invisible Man* Ellison drew on a wide range of experience, but his novel is not purely autobiographical. Ellison should not be identified with his unnamed narrator. But Ellison *uses* his personal experience imaginatively to create a remarkably inventive piece of fiction. He draws on his experience at Tuskegee to write the college chapters and his knowledge of the Communist party to write the Brotherhood chapters. He uses his rich and varied experience in Harlem as the basis for his description of street life in New York. Other sources for Ellison were his reading and the rich folk heritage of blacks. He uses the blues and jazz rhythms, folktales and jive talk, and characters drawn from frontier literature, as well as the tales he heard in the streets of Oklahoma City while growing up. The novel begins and ends with references to jazz musician Louis Armstrong singing, "What did I do/To be so black/And blue?"

One of the unusual things about *Invisible Man* is that it was immediately popular with both whites and blacks. Ellison has the rare ability in this novel to present a hero with whom people of diverse backgrounds can identify. Not only did the unnamed hero stand for the black man searching for his identity in a white world, but he seemed to represent to white college students *any* young man going through a crisis of values on his way to discovering himself. Readers on both sides of the Atlantic viewed *Invisible Man* as a work to be read alongside the popular plays and novels of Jean-Paul Sartre and Albert Camus.

During the 1960s the popularity of *Invisible Man* decreased, not so much with whites as with blacks. Many young black writers resented *Invisible Man*'s having been named the most distinguished novel of the past twenty years. They did not think that Ellison spoke for them because he was too much of an "Uncle Tom," a black who served the white man's interests. A generation accustomed to outspoken black leaders such as Malcolm X and Stokely Carmichael wanted its literature more radical. In the 1970s, many black poets and novelists emphasized the uniqueness of black life. Ellison refused to go in that direction. For him the core of America lay in the genuine integration of white and black.

"I don't recognize any white culture," he said to his friend, the black writer James Alan McPherson. "I recognize no American culture which is not the partial creation of black people. I recognize no American style in literature, in dance, in music, even in assembly-line processes, which does not bear the mark of the American Negro."

Ellison became a member of the American literary establishment. He taught at Bard College, Rutgers, the University of Chicago, and New York University. He served as a trustee of Bennington College. He became a member of the American Academy of Arts and Sciences and the National Institute of Arts and Letters. In 1964, he published a second book, *Shadow and Act*, a collection of essays about his personal life, as well as about literature, music, and the black experience in America. He worked on a second novel, about a black evangelist and a white orphan boy whom he has adopted. Parts of the novel were published as stories, but the complete novel had not been published by the mid-1980s.

And so Ralph Waldo Ellison remained a paradox. He had survived the criticism of the 1960s and 70s to become one of the most admired black American writers of the 1980s. At the same time he remained a one-novel man, and his admirers and critics alike wondered whether that second novel would ever be published.

Well, you could say, it may be all right being a one-novel man if the novel is as good as *Invisible Man*.

THE NOVEL

The Plot

Invisible Man opens with a Prologue. The un-named narrator tells you that he is an invisible man living in a hole under the streets of New York somewhere near Harlem. His hole is warm and bright. He has come here to hibernate, to think out the meaning of life, after the events he is about to narrate. What drove him to this state of hibernation? He begins to tell you.

The story starts when the narrator graduates from high school in a southern town. The leading white citizens invite him to give his graduation speech at a "smoker" in the ballroom of the local hotel. He arrives to find himself part of a "battle royal" in which local black boys are forced to fight one another blindfolded for the entertainment of the drunken whites. After the battle, the blacks are further humiliated by having to crawl on an electrified carpet to pick up coins. Finally, the hero is allowed to give his speech and is rewarded with a leather briefcase and a scholarship to the state college for blacks.

The narrator is a good student at college and is sufficiently well thought of to be allowed to drive distinguished white visitors around the campus and community. Near the end of his junior year he drives one of the trustees, a Mr. Norton, out into the country. They arrive by accident at the cabin of a black sharecropper named Jim Trueblood, who has caused a terrible scandal by committing incest with his daughter. Trueblood tells his story to Norton who is so overwhelmed that he nearly faints. In order to revive Norton, the narrator takes him for a drink to a nearby bar and house of prostitution called the Golden Day. A group of veterans who are patients at the local mental hospital arrive at the same time, and a wild brawl ensues during which Mr. Norton passes out. He is carried upstairs to one of the prostitute's rooms and revived by a veteran who was once a physician.

The horrified narrator finally returns Norton to the college, but the damage has been done. The young man is called into the president's office and dismissed from school. The president, Dr. Bledsoe, gives him letters of introduction to a number of the school's trustees in New York, and the narrator boards a bus the following day, hoping that the letters will help him succeed in the white world.

To his surprise the letters do not seem to help when he arrives in Harlem. No one offers him a job. Finally, young Mr. Emerson, the son of one of the trustees, explains why: The letters were not letters of recommendation at all but instructions *not* to help the boy, to keep him away from any further association with the college. The stunned narrator now has nowhere to turn, and so takes a job at the Liberty Paint Company at the recommendation of young Mr. Emerson. The experience is a bizarre one. He is sent to work with an old black man named Lucius Brockway. Brockway, a black man, is the real creator of the Optic White paint that Liberty is so proud of, but the naive young narrator doesn't understand the irony of the situation.

Later, when he fails to pay attention to Brockway's instructions, he is knocked out in an explosion. When he wakes up, he finds himself in a large glass and metal box in the factory hospital. He seems to be the object of some sort of psychological experiment. He is subjected to electric shock treatment, questioned, given a new name by a man in a white coat, and released. Dazed, he returns to Harlem like a newborn infant, unable to care for himself.

The confused protagonist is taken in by a compassionate black woman named Mary Rambo, who nurses him back to health. But what is he to do? Winter is coming and the money given him in compensation by the factory has all but run out. The narrator goes out into the icy streets and has the most important experience of his life. He sees an old black couple being evicted and spontaneously gets up before the gathered crowd and stirs the people to action. He has found a new identity—as a spokesman for blacks—but the police arrive and he is forced to flee across the rooftops, followed by a white man who introduces himself as Brother Jack. Brother Jack would like the narrator to work for his organization, the Brotherhood, as a speaker for the Harlem district. The narrator hesitates, then accepts the offer. He is given a new name and is moved from Harlem to a new location, where he will study the literature of the Brotherhood.

The next evening the narrator is taken to Harlem to begin his career as a speaker for the Brotherhood. He and several others sit on a platform in a large arena, and he is the last to speak. When he speaks, he electrifies the audience with his emotional power, but the Brotherhood is not pleased. They consider his style primitive and backward, and so he is barred from further speeches until he has been trained by Brother Hambro in the methods and teachings of the Brotherhood.

Four months later the narrator is made chief spokesman of the Harlem district. His committee, which includes Brother Tobitt, Brother Tarp, and the narrator's favorite, Brother Tod Clifton, is concerned about regaining the support of the community from Ras the Exhorter, a wild black-nationalist rabble-rouser who has drawn black people into a war with whites. The narrator and his new friend Clifton engage in a street fight with Ras, a fight that foreshadows the final battle in the novel between the Brotherhood and supporters of the black nationalist. Nothing is concluded, but at the same time Ras is unable to stop the Brotherhood, under the narrator's leadership, from making great progress in Harlem.

Brother Tarp, as a token of his support for the narrator's leadership, gives him a link of leg chain. But there are many in the Brotherhood who do not like the narrator. He is too successful and moving too fast. At a meeting of the committee, the narrator is removed from a leadership role in Harlem and ordered to lecture downtown on the Woman Question. He is stunned, but he obeys the Brotherhood and gives the lecture as ordered, whereupon a white woman, more interested in his sexuality as a black man than in the Woman Question, seduces him in her apartment after the lecture. His lectures downtown continue until he is suddenly and surprisingly returned to Harlem after the unexpected disappearance of Brother Tod Clifton.

The narrator returns to Harlem, hoping to reorganize the neighborhood, but things have deteriorated since he was sent downtown. He searches for Tod Clifton and finds him, pathetically selling Black Sambo dolls near the New York Public Library. A police officer nabs Clifton for illegal peddling and shoots him when he resists arrest. Suddenly the narrator, who has witnessed this, finds himself plunged into an historical event. A huge funeral is arranged for Clifton in Harlem, and the narrator speaks at the occasion, but his speech is very different from his earlier speeches. He can no longer rouse the crowd to action. He returns to Brotherhood headquarters and is severely criticized by Brother Jack for having acted without authority.

The angry narrator is frustrated at his inability to accomplish anything constructive. He puts on a pair of sunglasses to disguise himself and suddenly finds that he has taken on another new identity, that of Rinehart, a swindler. Not even Ras the Exhorter, now Ras the Destroyer, seems to recognize the narrator in this disguise. Concerned about the growing strength of Ras and his men, the narrator goes for advice to Brother Hambro's. Here he is told that international policies have temporarily changed directives. Harlem is no longer a priority for the Brotherhood. The narrator is astonished. Again he has been betrayed by an organization he trusted. He finally begins to see what a fool he has been and understands that he has, to white people, been invisible. He follows his grandfather's advice and starts "yessing them to death," meanwhile secretly planning his own strategy.

As a part of his revenge he spends a drunken evening with Sybil, the wife of one of the Brotherhood members, hoping to obtain useful information from her. But she is more interested in his body than in politics. A telephone call interrupts them. There is a huge riot in the district, and the narrator is needed. He hurries back to Harlem to find total chaos. Looters are everywhere, and Ras and his troops are out in force. Ras, on a black horse and dressed as an Ethiopian chieftain, is armed with spear and shield. The narrator narrowly escapes being killed by Ras. He dives into a manhole to avoid being mugged by a group of white thugs, and falls asleep.

He wakes up to find himself in a dark, underground passage from which he can't escape, and decides to stay. Here he will try to understand what has happened to him and then write his story. The novel ends with an Epilogue in which the narrator decides it is time to come out of his hole. He is ready to rejoin society, because he knows and understands himself now "The hibernation is over. I must shake off the old skin and come up for breath," he says. The novel ends as he makes a new beginning.

The Characters
MAJOR CHARACTER

The Narrator

You begin with a problem. The novel's central character has no name. Some readers refer to him as the Invisible Man, others call him the narrator. Some regard him as the protagonist or the hero. You may call him by any of these titles, because he has all these roles.

"I am an invisible man," he tells you in the first sentence of the novel. When he calls himself invisible, he means that other people don't see him, that no one recognizes him as a person, as an individual. A helpful way to understand the Invisible Man as a character is to use the ideas of the noted twentieth-century Jewish philosopher, Martin Buber. Buber distinguishes between I-Thou relationships and I-It relationships. When we love someone, there is an I-Thou relationship, one between two individuals who truly care for one another as persons. In an I-It relationship we use others as things. We like people for what we can get out of them.

If you apply this idea to Ellison's central character, you may conclude that he is invisible because people always see him as an "It," never as a "Thou." He is used by the college officials and the wealthy white trustees in the first half of the novel and by the leaders of the Brotherhood in the second half. Once he is no longer useful to these people, he is discarded like trash. It is particularly interesting to note that, when people want to use him, they give him a name. He is named in Chapter 11 by the doctors at the factory hospital before being released. He is renamed by the Brotherhood in Chapter 14. Notice that you are never told these names. The only name he is ever called is "Rinehart," and that is in Chapter 23 when he puts on a pair of dark glasses, and, later, a hat, to disguise himself from Ras the Exhorter's men. Throughout the chapter, he is mistaken for a variety of "Rineharts"—Rinehart, the gambler; Rinehart, the lover; Reverend Rinehart, the mininster. Eventually the protagonist discards the glasses, but it is significant that it is *his* choice, not someone else's. When the main events of the novel are over, he chooses to stay underground, to remain literally invisible— out of circulation—until he has thought through who he is and who *he* wants to be rather than accepting other people's definitions of him. At the end he decides to come out of his hole and rejoin society. Maybe he will still be invisible. That is an interesting point for you to consider. Ellison certainly seems ambiguous about it in the Epilogue. But the narrator is a different person from the young man who experienced the adventures in the main body of the novel.

The Invisible Man is not only the chief actor in the novel—the protagonist—he is also its narrator. The story is told in the first person, and for that reason you have to be careful about the way you interpret it. In this guide's section on Point of View you will find additional material on the problems of interpreting first-person narratives. For now, you need to be aware of the way in which first-person narration affects your analysis of the Invisible Man as a character. The Invisible Man is what is known as a *naive narrator*. Throughout most of the novel, he is young, inexperienced, and gullible. You cannot take what he says at face value because there are many, many occasions when he misses the irony of a situation or the true import of people's words and actions. Sometimes he simply misinterprets things. So he is not only a naive narrator, he is an *unreliable* narrator in the sense that you cannot trust his version of the story to be entirely accurate. He tells it as he sees it, but he doesn't always see it very well.

But, before you judge the narrator too quickly, be careful. He is not the same person at the end of the novel that he is at the beginning. He is a character who grows. The German word Bildungsroman is often used to describe the novel of education, the story of a person's growth to maturity. *Invisible Man* is a Bildungsroman, and the narrator changes a good deal during the course of the story. You will follow his development step by step in The Story section of this guide. For now, you should be aware that the protagonist is a developing rather than a static character. The only tricky thing to watch out for is that the Prologue represents a stage of development *after* the events of Chapters 1 to 25. Thus, if you are tracing the narrator's development, the order would be Chapters 1 to 25, Prologue, Epilogue. Between the Prologue and the Epilogue the narrator is actually *writing* the novel, and in the Epilogue he is trying to understand the meaning of what he's just done.

One final point: The narrator is an Afro-American. Part of the reason he's invisible is that Ellison feels white people do not *see* black people. Much of what he suffers comes at the hands of white people and those blacks who work for white people. From this point of view the narrator may be interpreted as a symbol for the black person in America. And if you are black or Hispanic, or a member of another minority that suffers from prejudice, you may identify especially with this character, who seems to be treated so unjustly at the hands of prejudiced men and women. But Ralph Ellison, when asked about the narrator, frequently emphasized the point that his hero was universal—he was any person searching for identity in the chaos and complexity of contemporary America.

OTHER CHARACTERS

Invisible Man is, in a sense, a one-character novel. The narrator himself is the *only* figure whose life you are concerned with from the beginning to the end of the novel. Other people enter the novel, live in it for a few chapters as they influence the narrator, then vanish. We will look briefly at the most important of these figures in the order that they appear in the book. Each of these characters is also discussed in some detail in the appropriate chapters of The Story section. You should consult those chapters for more complete treatment. The minor figures are considered briefly in the Notes in The Story section.

Mr. Norton (Chapter 2)

Mr. Norton (his name suggests northern) is the first figure to influence the narrator's destiny. He is a white-haired, red-faced multimillionaire from Boston who serves on the black college's Board of Trustees. He looks and acts like Santa Claus, seeing himself as a good-natured benefactor of black people. Norton tells the narrator that he was one of the college's founders and that his success as a man depends on the success of the college's students. He seems to mean by this that black people ought to try and rise up from the effects of slavery and illiteracy in the way prescribed by the white power structure.

The narrator drives Mr. Norton out to the country, where they stop at the home of a black share-cropper named James Trueblood, who has committed incest with his daughter. Norton seems both horrified and fascinated by Trueblood's story and is so shocked by hearing it that he must be taken to a bar named the Golden Day for a drink to revive him. Here he is injured in a scuffle, eventually revived, and finally returned to the college, but not before the damage has been done—Norton has been educated to the realities of black life in the South.

He has seen not what Dr. Bledsoe, the college president, wants him to see but what black people like Jim Trueblood and the veterans at the Golden Day really think and feel about themselves and whites. In the process he is exposed as a vulnerable old man who is himself near death and needs care. Who cares for him? A prostitute and a supposedly crazy black veteran. Has the narrator intentionally taken Mr. Norton on a journey to self-knowledge?

Dr. Bledsoe (Chapter 4)

On his way back from the Golden Day, the narrator says, "Here within this quiet greenness I possessed the only identity I had ever known, and I was losing it." That identity is associated with Dr. Bledsoe, the president of the college. "He was the example of everything I hoped to be," the narrator tells us. Bledsoe is rich, he has a beautiful wife, and he owns two Cadillac automobiles. He is a successful and powerful black man in a white man's world.

Do you see the two sides of Bledsoe that the narrator misses? There is the surface Bledsoe humbly attending to his white guests and doing exactly what white people expect of a black man. You can see this Bledsoe especially in Chapter 5, the vespers sequence. There is also the Bledsoe who bitterly attacks the narrator for taking Mr. Norton to Jim Trueblood's and the Golden Day, the Bledsoe who will attack anybody and anything to hold on to the power which he has. This is the Bledsoe who "bleeds his people so," as his name suggests—the Bledsoe that the narrator can't let himself believe in. Ellison depicts Bledsoe as a man who rather than really helping his race is actually holding it back. Do you agree?

Young Mr. Emerson (Chapter 9)

Young Mr. Emerson is the son of the trustee to whom the seventh of Bledsoe's sealed letters is addressed. Young Emerson opens the letter and explains to the shocked narrator what the letters have really said. Do you admire young Mr. Emerson for this action? It seems like a step forward in the narrator's development. After all, he cannot grow until he stops idealizing people like Norton and Bledsoe. Emerson's decision to tell him the truth may enable him to take a step forward.

The question remains: What does Emerson offer him in place of the world of Bledsoe and the college? Read Chapter 9 carefully and look at the details of young Mr. Emerson's world—a world of nightclubs like the Club Calamus (named for Walt Whitman's "Calamus" poems, a group of openly homosexual poems), a world of jazz joints in Greenwich Village and Harlem where blacks and whites can mingle. Young Mr. Emerson thinks of himself as Huckleberry Finn and he thinks of blacks as being like Jim. Just as Huck in Mark Twain's novel decides not to turn Jim in, so young Mr. Emerson feels that he is helping the narrator by freeing him from the slavery of ignorance. Do you believe Emerson is really helping the narrator? What are his motives? Are they clear?

In thinking about him, you may wish to consider the symbolism of his name. Remember that Ralph Ellison was named after Ralph Waldo Emerson. Biographical information on the historical Emerson may be found in a Note to Chapter 9. Is there a parallel between young Mr. Emerson and the famous nineteenth-century essayist? Have you read "The American Scholar" or "Self Reliance"? What might the author of these essays say about young

Mr. Emerson? Have Ralph Waldo Emerson's ideas been diluted and corrupted over time?

Mary Rambo (Chapter 12)

After his shattering experiences in the paint factory in Chapters 10 and 11, the narrator returns to Harlem but is too weak to care for himself. The person who saves his life is Mary Rambo. Mary is important in the novel because she starts the narrator on the right track by offering him love and care without asking anything in return. She doesn't expect him to *be* something for her. The fact that the narrator has been living at Men's House, a place where important blacks gather to impress one another, is significant. After the paint factory experience, the narrator is like a newborn child. He cannot survive at Men's House. He needs a mother to care for him, and Mary Rambo serves that role. She feeds him, shelters him, and gives him love. She is part of that important southern folk tradition that the narrator has abandoned, the tradition of the relatively uneducated but morally upright southern black mother. The narrator has come to believe he is too good for such people. He traveled to New York to make his way among whites and educated blacks. He has had nothing to do with the servants, farmers, and housekeepers of his childhood in the South. Mary reminds him of those true values he has forgotten. "I'm in New York but New York ain't in me," she tells him. "Don't git corrupted." He calls her "a force, a stable, familiar force like something out of my past which kept me from whirling off into some unknown. . . ."

Though he leaves Mary's, what she stands for remains so important to him that, at the end of

Chapter 25, when he is nearly killed in the street riot, he tries to get back to Mary's, where he can be loved and cared for. But he never does. Instead he remains in the hole that becomes his new home, his new room or womb. Do you see parallels between his room at Mary's and the underground hole?

Brother Jack (Chapter 13)

In Chapter 13 the narrator makes a powerful speech at a sidewalk eviction. The speech attracts the attention of "a short insignificant bushy-eyebrowed, white man with red hair." The man is Brother Jack, the leader of the Brotherhood, who dominates the narrator's life for the next ten chapters. It is not until the crucial showdown between the narrator and Brother Jack in Chapter 22, after the funeral of Tod Clifton, that the narrator finally *sees* the truth about Brother Jack, a truth that is vividly symbolized by Brother Jack's glass eye, which drops out of its socket into a glass of water during the argument. You might want to explore the symbolism of the glass eye further.

Brother Jack's red hair may stand for his Communist ideology, just as the Brotherhood may represent the Communist party, to which Ellison and other black writers and thinkers were drawn during the 1930s. Certainly the sequence of events in Chapters 13 to 22 roughly parallels the relationships between many black American intellectuals and the Communists during the Depression and the early years of World War II. Jack, as the leader, expresses much of the party's ideology.

If you wish to pursue the study of Brother Jack as a symbol of communism in America during the 1930s, remember that a good many leftist writers and critics did not like Ellison's portrayal of Brother Jack and thought the chapters about the Brotherhood the weakest section of the novel (see The Critics section of this guide for some examples of their reaction). Whether you agree with them or not, Brother Jack is a character who merits close study.

His name, Jack, is a common slang term for money, and money is what attracts the narrator to Brother Jack in the first place. He uses the money to pay Mary Rambo, to buy new clothes, and to move into a social set that includes wealthy white women. The name "Jack" combined with Jack's glass eye also suggests the "one-eyed Jacks" in playing cards. Jack pretends to be the king of the Brotherhood in New York, but when the real international kings make changes in policy, Jack turns out to be nothing more than a discard. Do you see any parallels between Jack and Bledsoe, those two figures who dominate the narrator's life throughout the better part of the novel?

Brother Tod Clifton (Chapter 17)

In Chapter 17 the narrator is made the chief spokesman of the Harlem District for the Brotherhood, and at his first meeting he is introduced by Brother Jack to Brother Tod Clifton. Clifton is tall, black, and strikingly handsome. This young, muscular man is passionately engaged in his work. As a Harlem youth leader, he is sympathetic to the narrator's idea of organizing community leaders to fight evictions. The two begin their crusade as true brothers in the cause, and their friendship deepens when they end up literally fighting side by side against Ras the Exhorter, the militant black nationalist, and his men. Ras both hates and loves Tod.

He hates him because Tod works with white men, but he loves him because he is black and beautiful. He doesn't kill Tod, because he hopes that Tod will some day join his cause.

Tod Clifton is one of the genuinely loveable and tragic figures in the novel. He is the hope of the black community. His intelligence, physical grace, strength and cunning on the streets, as well as his loyalty to his people, make him a hero. Then, without warning, he disappears from the district. The narrator does not know why, because it is during the time that the narrator himself has been exiled from Harlem. The narrator returns to the district in Chapter 20 and begins his search for Tod. And he finds him, not in Harlem, but downtown near the main building of the New York Public Library, hawking Sambo dolls. What did Ellison have in mind by making Tod a mockery of himself, a mockery of everything that he and the narrator have stood for in Harlem?

If you are going to deal with Tod as a character, this is the first important question you must answer. Reread Chapter 20 carefully and look for clues. Perhaps Tod left Harlem because the Brotherhood betrayed him and changed its emphasis to national and international issues. Perhaps he gave up because he realized, as the narrator finally does, that the Brotherhood was just using him. What is your interpretation, at this point in the novel, of Tod's role?

Suddenly the ludicrous comedy of Tod's part as a sidewalk peddler turns into a tragedy. Tod is shot and killed by a white policeman for resisting arrest. Again you must ask, "Why"? Is Tod's death primarily the result of social forces, of white prejudice, of police brutality? Or does Tod in a sense take his own life? Would it help you to know that the German word for "death" is "Tod"? Does this name have particular symbolic importance in the novel? If so, what? Even if the name Tod suggests death, it still does not answer the question of why Tod must die.

Tod's death has a powerful impact on the narrator. His friendship with Tod evokes a moving and terrible grief, which he tries to put into words at Tod's huge outdoor funeral. Tod Clifton, in death, becomes a symbol for all black people, for all the young and talented black people who are symbolically shot down in all sorts of ways. Tod is dead, and the narrator moves the crowd to grief. But he cannot move them to political action. He can, however, rouse himself to human action against the Brotherhood which destroyed Tod. Tod Clifton is the catalyst for the narrator's final awakening to self in Chapters 22 and 23. In that role, Tod is one of the truly important figures in the novel.

Brother Tarp and Brother Wrestrum (Chapters 17 and 18)

At the same time that the narrator meets Tod Clifton, he also meets two other black brothers, Brother Tarp, who becomes an inspiration to him, and Brother Wrestrum, who becomes a Judas figure. They may symbolize two equal and opposite reactions to the black situation—one good, the other evil.

Tarp is a genuine freedom fighter. Like his hero, Frederick Douglass (see the Note to Chapter 17), whose picture he puts over the narrator's desk, Tarp has been cruelly punished for fighting tyranny. "I said no to a man who wanted to take something from me," and for saying *no* he was sentenced to nineteen years at hard labor. So he broke his chains, outran the dogs, headed north, and joined the Brotherhood because it seemed like a good place to be in his fight for freedom. He is old, and as a symbol of his age, he gives the narrator the piece of chain which he had filed from his leg and saved. For Tarp this is a way of passing on the fight to the younger generation. Tarp, the narrator realizes, reminds him of his own grandfather, whose image has haunted him since his childhood.

The narrator keeps Tarp's leg iron on his desk as a reminder of the fight against slavery in which they are all involved. He is stirred and reassured by the gift, which he later puts into his briefcase and uses as a weapon of self-defense during the riot described in the final chapters.

Brother Wrestrum sees the leg iron on the narrator's desk and complains about it. He is a "pure brother," and he wants no reminders of the black man's past in the office. He wants all Brotherhood members to wear buttons or pins so that they can be instantly recognized. Wrestrum is not working for black freedom, but for the Brotherhood, and he is perfectly willing to turn against any black member who does not follow Brotherhood discipline to the letter. It seems as if Wrestrum is a kind of paid spy for the higher-ups like Brother Jack. After all, it is Brother Wrestrum who turns the narrator in to the board, charging him with selfish opportunism and causing him to be sent downtown to lecture on the Woman Question. Is Brother Wrestrum acting on his own initiative when he accuses the narrator in the middle of Chapter 18, or is he acting on orders? You don't know, but in either case there is something consistently sneaky and dishonest about Brother Wrestrum, whose name sounds unmistakably like "rest room." In Chapter 24 the narrator refers to him as "that out-house Wrestrum." Need anything more be said?

Ras the Exhorter (Chapter 17)

Ras the Exhorter enters the novel with Tod Clifton in Chapter 17 but survives Tod's death to become the most dominant figure in the book's closing chapters. Ras the Exhorter, who becomes Ras the Destroyer during the final race riot, is a black na-tionalist who has organized the Harlem commu-nity along racial lines. The name "Ras" clearly sug-gests "race." The name may also come from "Ra," the name of the Egyptian sun-god, who is pictured as a man with a hawk's head. Literally, the name comes from the Amharic word *Ras*, which means "prince" or "king." The Ethiopian emperor Haile Selassie was Ras Tafari before he became emperor, and the Jamaica-based religion Rastafarianism be-lieves that its members derive their ancestry from Ethiopia and, if traced all the way back, to Solo-mon and the Queen of Sheba. Rastafarian ideas were well known in Harlem during Ellison's time. Ras is inspiring because he has a message that blacks want to listen to, the unity of race. On the other hand, he is terrifying, because his methods are vio-lent and lead finally to the terrible reality of black fighting against black in senseless mutual destruc-tion. When the Brotherhood is no longer inter-ested in Harlem, they turn it over to Ras, who uses the pretext of Tod Clifton's death to start a race riot. What Ellison seems to be suggesting through Ras is that the ultimate implications of Ras' phi-losophy are totally self-destructive. Ras and the

Brotherhood appear to be equally wrong choices for different reasons.

One of the unusual things about Ellison's portrait of Ras is that it is not based on any particular figure. Ellison was asked if he had Marcus Garvey in mind, because Garvey was a black nationalist from Jamaica who spoke with a Caribbean accent similar to the one Ras uses in *Invisible Man*. Ellison said that Ras came from his imagination. Rather than being historical, the figure of Ras is prophetic. Within fifteen years after *Invisible Man* was published, figures like Ras sprang up all over America. Some, like Malcolm X, became Black Muslims. Others, like Huey Newton and Eldridge Cleaver, called themselves Black Panthers and carried weapons, as they said, to defend themselves against white violence. America's cities—Watts (Los Angeles), Detroit, Newark, Chicago—were rocked with race riots, and many blacks turned away from any kind of dialog with whites. Today the figure of Ras, and the riot at the end of the novel which he engenders and prolongs, seem to prophesy what America would go through in the 1960s when the calmer voices of integration gave way to the radical shouts of the Black Muslims and Pan-African movements. Ras is a powerful and frightening figure who may symbolize some of Ellison's worst fears.

Rinehart (Chapter 23)

Rinehart is a student's dream. Almost anything you say about him is likely to be true. About Rinehart there are far more questions than answers, and you should have an exciting time exploring this mysterious figure who never appears.

You know that someone or perhaps several people named Rinehart exist, because the narrator is mistaken for Rinehart a number of times in Chapter 23 after he puts on a pair of dark glasses and a white hat to disguise himself from Ras the Exhorter's men. The glasses and the hat are magical. "They see the hat, not me. There is magic in it. It hides me right in front of their eyes . . ." the narrator thinks to himself. Not only does it hide him, it gives him a new identity, another new identity—that of a man named Rinehart who, it seems, is a numbers runner, a lover, a storefront evangelist, and a hipster. But can one man be all these things at once? Could there be at least two or three Rineharts? Is Rinehart a character at all? Is he really more a symbol, a type, than an individual?

The narrator thinks about the meaning of Rinehart's name. "Could he himself be both rind and heart? What is real anyway?" Later he says, "So I'd accept it, I'd explore it, rine and heart." If we are trying to discover the meaning of Rinehart as a symbol, we need to look at both the words "rind" and "rine." "Rind" means a thick outer skin, like the rind of an orange. It means a kind of toughness that enables one to survive. "Rine" is really street talk for "rind." A man with a lot of "rine" is a tough dude, one who can survive in the chaos and confusion of the unstructured world of the street. Ellison said in an interview that "Rinehart is my name for the personification of chaos. He is also intended to represent America and change. He has lived so long with chaos that he knows how to manipulate it."

Rinehart is a con man, a manipulator. He lives in the world, but he doesn't really do anything for the world except use it. The identity of Rinehart may be a temporary sanctuary for the narrator, but it is another identity he must reject if he is to find himself as a person. Eventually he discards the glasses and the hat and takes to his hole to think out his true identity. You will have a fascinating time following the glasses and the hat through Chapters 23 to 25 and exploring what they suggest symbolically about the elusive and ever-present Mr. Rinehart, and the narrator's adoption of his life-style. Early in Chapter 25 the glasses are broken, and the narrator must face Ras the Destroyer without the protection of Rinehart. What might that suggest?

Other Elements
SETTING

Setting is always important in *Invisible Man*, because Ellison is both a realistic writer and a symbolist. He puts events in real settings, but these settings always stand for something beyond themselves.

The largest and most significant element in setting is the contrast between South and North. Chapters 1 to 6 take place in the South, Chapters 8 to 25 in the North, with Chapter 7 as a transition. In Ellison's words, the narrator "leaves the South and goes North; this, as you will notice in reading Negro folktales, is always the road to freedom." Thus one major pattern of the novel is a move from the restricting bonds of the South, symbolized by the rigid distinctions between black and white, to the greater flexibility of the North as symbolized by life in Harlem. But the existence of that pattern should not lead you to view North and South *simply* as symbols for restriction and freedom. In Ellison's popular short story, "King of the Bingo Game," the anonymous narrator finds himself in the cold, unfriendly North missing the warmth and easygoing quality of southern life. Do you find, as you read *Invisible Man*, that North and South are mixed symbols, representing a variety of things? Is the South both restrictive *and* friendly, the North freer yet more impersonal?

There are several significant settings within each geographic area. The settings in Chapters 1 to 6 include the hotel ballroom where the battle royal takes place (Chapter 1), Jim Trueblood's farm (Chapter 2), the Golden Day (Chapter 3) and the college (Chapters 4 to 6). Each of these settings allows you to see black life in the South from a different perspective. Chapter 1 represents blacks in their most demeaning situation—on public display in the white world. Chapters 2 and 3 show blacks acting more freely in more natural settings, but these are settings outlawed for the college boys. The college boys are being educated on a tree-lined campus with brick buildings. It is a neat and orderly world, a world in which blacks are restricted to the kind of behavior that suits those black leaders who would please wealthy whites. The campus is an Uncle Tom world, a world of blacks trying to act like whites.

To grow, the narrator must stop idealizing this world and its leaders. He must accept the freer and yet more dangerous world symbolized by New York. New York is a microcosm of the North. Though not rigidly segregated like the South, it is divided into predominantly black Harlem and predominantly white downtown. Downtown is where the Brotherhood has its main office. It is where the narrator visits white "brothers and sisters." It is where Tod Clifton is killed by a white policeman. It is significant that when the narrator joins the Brotherhood, he leaves his rooms at Mary Rambo's boarding house in Harlem to take more expensive rooms in a white part of town. Harlem is the center of black life and culture, the place where Ellison himself lived for a number of years after leaving Tuskegee Institute in Alabama. The black must know and understand Harlem in order to find his identity. By rejecting Harlem, the narrator has rejected his own blackness. He has spent most of the novel trying to become white.

The final significant setting is the underground cave of the Prologue and Epilogue. Here, the narrator is in a "border area," not associated with either black or white. Here he has retreated into himself to think out his identity, to come to some self-understanding. Here, alone, apart from those who try to force identity on him, he is able to arrive at some genuine self-knowledge. The cave is a place of contemplation, a place to grow a new skin and be protected from the harsh realities of the outside world until he is strong enough to go outside. The novel ends, significantly, with the narrator's decision to leave the cave, to go up and out into the real world again, a world of both blacks and whites.

STYLE

Invisible Man is a stylistic performance of the highest order, a delight and a constant series of surprises to anyone who loves words. That's one view. The other is that it is a confusing mass of shifting styles that only serves to keep the reader from knowing what's going on. Therefore, take this section of the study guide as a warning: *Invis-*

ible Man is not an easy novel to read, and if you want to get the maximum pleasure and understanding from Ellison's dazzling use of language, you will have to work at it.

Ellison's first stylistic device is word play. He loves puns, rhymes, slogans, and paradoxes. "I yam what I am!" cries the narrator, after buying a hot buttered yam from a street vendor in Chapter 13. "If It's Optic White, It's the Right White" is a slogan for the Liberty Paint Factory coined by the black Lucius Brockway. It reminds the narrator of the old southern expression, "If you're white, you're right." "All it takes to get along in this here man's town is a little shit, grit, and mother-wit," says Peter Wheatstraw, a street blues singer in Harlem. What all these expressions and many others have in common is that they are not only funny and clever, they also embody folk wisdom that the narrator needs to hear and understand.

Ellison also has a fine ear for all kinds of speech—especially varieties of black folk dialect. All the black folk characters—Jim Trueblood, Burnside the Vet, Brockway, Wheatstraw, Mary Rambo, Brother Tarp, and at the end the two black revolutionaries Scofield and Dupree—speak in their own varieties of black folk dialect and exhibit a kind of knowledge that the more educated "white" characters seem to lack, a "street" knowledge that has passed from South to North, from generation to generation, and needs to be remembered.

Ellison's stylistic range is enormous. In Chapter 2 he writes a description of the college in the style of the poet T. S. Eliot. In Chapter 4 he writes a sermon modeled on the classic oratory of black preachers throughout the South in the early twentieth century. Influenced by a range of writers from

Eliot and Joyce to Dostoevsky and Richard Wright, he can write in whatever style suits his purpose at the time. When asked about his changing styles in the novel, he said, "In the South, when he [the narrator] was trying to fit into a traditional pattern and where his sense of certainty had not yet been challenged, I felt a more naturalistic treatment was adequate. . . . As the hero passes from the South to the North, from the relatively stable to the swiftly changing, his sense of certainty is lost and the style becomes expressionistic. Later on during his fall from grace in the Brotherhood it becomes some-what surrealistic. The styles try to express both his state of consciousness and the state of society."

You might underline the three words *naturalistic*, *expressionistic*, and *surrealistic*. If Ellison is right in his analysis, then these are the three major styles of the novel. "Naturalistic" means faithful to the small details of outward reality or nature. "Expressionistic" means characters and actions standing for inner states. "Surrealistic" means tending to deal with the world of dreams and the unconscious. Thus, the scenes at the college are naturalistic, the scenes at the paint factory are expressionistic, and the scenes from the Harlem riot chapters at the end are surrealistic. We will explore the significance of these stylistic shifts more fully in The Story section. For now you may want to think about *why* Ellison felt that realism alone was not enough. What could these other styles do for him that realism could not?

POINT OF VIEW

Invisible Man is a first-person narrative told by a developing character. That means you can trust his perceptions and judgments much more toward the end of the novel than you can at the beginning.

At the beginning (leaving out the Prologue, which we will look at later with the Epilogue) the narrator is young and naive. In Chapter 1 he is a high school graduate. In Chapters 2 to 6 he is a college junior. He has experienced little of the real world. As a result he misinterprets, misses ironies, and makes naive judgments about other characters. Your interpretation of the events of the first third of the novel must be colored by your awareness that the narrator is frequently missing the point. You must be more mature and perceptive than he is.

During Chapters 7 to 10, his first months in New York, he is not much better, but the accident in the paint factory at the end of Chapter 10 changes him. In Chapters 11 to 13 you see a more thoughtful narrator emerge from the machine in the paint factory hospital. He begins to ask questions about his identity, makes some connection with his black roots, and discovers his vocation when he makes an eloquent speech protesting the eviction of an old couple from their apartment. As the narrator becomes more concerned with social justice, you may find yourself identifying more strongly with him. But he still has a long way to go.

In Chapters 14 to 21, the period when he is working for the Brotherhood, he is mature in some ways but not in others. The narrator's sight begins to clear in Chapter 22, when he sees many of the Brotherhood members for what they really are for the first time. Chapter 23, in which he discovers the identity of Rinehart, marks another phase of his development, and the Prologue and Epilogue, which happen chronologically *after* the action of the novel proper, represent a final phase.

Your job as a reader is to sort out this progress as it occurs and to evaluate how much the ideas of the narrator at any particular stage of his development may be associated with those of the author. Is the narrator, as he nears maturity in the later chapters, speaking for Ellison? Do the Prologue and Epilogue, more than the main body of the novel, represent an identification between narrator and author? A look at Ellison's essays in *Shadow and Act* (1964) would help you answer these questions. "That Same Pain, That Same Pleasure" is particularly helpful. Some critics, Marcus Klein for one (see "The Critics"), feel that Ellison violates point of view in the Epilogue by making the narrator come to conclusions that are too optimistic, too affirmative for his character. These statements, say the critics, are really more Ellison's than the narrator's, and they belong in a different novel. You will have to make your own decision about these questions as you study the Epilogue to the novel.

THEMES

The following are major themes of *Invisible Man*.

1. INVISIBILITY

The most natural theme to begin with is that of invisibility. What is an invisible man? How is the kind of invisibility Ellison writes about different from the physical invisibility of the English writer H. G. Wells' famous book *The Invisible Man*? A reading of Ellison's novel suggests that the theme of invisibility has different dimensions: (a) Invisibility suggests the unwillingness of others to see the individual as a person. The narrator is invisible because people see in him only what they want to see, not what he really is. Invisibility, in this sense, has a strong sense of racial prejudice. White people often do not *see* black people as individual human beings. (b) Invisibility suggests separation from society. While the narrator is in his hole, he is invisible. He cannot be seen by society. He is invisible because he chooses to remain apart. Invisibility, in this sense, is associated with hibernation, with the narrator's conscious choice to remain in his cave and think. (c) Invisibility suggests lack of self-hood. A person is invisible if he has no self, no identity. This leads you to the second theme.

2.   THE SEARCH FOR IDENTITY
"Who am I?" This phrase echoes through the novel, especially in Chapters 12 and 23, those crucial sequences where the narrator struggles most openly with the problem of identity. The narrator has no name. At various points in the novel he is given pieces of paper by individuals or groups. These pieces of paper name him, identify him as having some role: student, patient, member of the Brotherhood. Yet none of these names is really *his*. The narrator cannot be named until he has a self, a self that is not defined by outside groups and organizations. The story of *Invisible Man*, then, might be described as the narrator's taking on and discarding a whole series of false identities, each one bringing him a little closer to a true sense of self.

3.   BLACK VS WHITE
This is both a very simple and an enormously complex theme. On a simple level *Invisible Man* is a novel about race in America, about the way in which black people suffer from the prejudice of white people and from the cruelty of other black people who want to please white people. But the

symbols of black and white are used also in more complex fashion. Traditionally, in Western culture black symbolizes evil, and white stands for good. Ellison plays with this symbolism in *Invisible Man*, turning it inside out and upside down. The narrator, for example, at first tries to deny his blackness, but eventually plunges into a dark hole—a *black* hole—where he remains for a long time. What is the true relationship between black and white? The expressionistic sequence at Liberty Paints in Chapter 10 is built almost entirely on the interplay between black and white as symbols. If black and white are mixed, what are the results? Can they be kept separate? Should blacks try to be like whites? If not, why not? These are all questions raised by Ellison's fascinating use of the black-white conflict in this novel.

4. FROM IGNORANCE TO KNOWLEDGE

Invisible Man might be read as a novel about a young man's journey from ignorance to knowledge. Early in the novel, the naive narrator knows little. He is constantly taken in by people's appearances. As he goes through the series of initiations from the battle royal in Chapter 1 to the humiliating exposure by young Mr. Emerson in Chapter 9, to the experiences with the Brotherhood in the later chapters, he gains more and more insight. You might notice that ignorance is often associated with blindness and knowledge with sight, ignorance with darkness and knowledge with light. The narrator falls into a dark hole, but he fills it with light, with 1,369 light bulbs. If you explore this theme fully, you will see that it parallels and interrelates with the black vs white theme.

5.   THE WISDOM OF THE BLACK FOLK EXPERIENCE

Robert G. O'Meally's fine book, *The Craft of Ralph Ellison*, focuses on this important theme (see The Critics section of this guide for an excerpt). He notes how important the black folk tradition is in *Invisible Man*. This tradition includes blues (Louis Armstrong singing "What Did I Do to Be So Black and Blue?"), spirituals, sermons of southern ministers, folktales (especially the Uncle Remus stories), jive talk, street language, colloquial speech of southern blacks like Jim Trueblood, the down-home wisdom of Mary Rambo, and all sorts of traditional verbal games.

Look for these elements as you read the novel and notice that the narrator frequently either ignores or looks down on the people who embody or preserve these traditions. To the extent that he tries to be white, to be upper class, the narrator forgets his black folk heritage and the common-sense wisdom that goes with it. It is only when he accepts this source of knowledge and culture that he can become a real human being.

FORM AND STRUCTURE

Form and structure do not pose a problem in this otherwise complex novel. The form is simple: It is chronological narrative with no flashbacks and no confusing time switches. The only formal element that might give you any trouble is Ellison's use of the Prologue and Epilogue. The Prologue, which precedes Chapter 1, occurs in time after the action of Chapters 1 to 25 has been completed, but before the Epilogue. In the novel proper, Chapters 1 to 25, the narrator tells you what he did to end up in the "hole" which he describes in the Prologue. In the Epilogue he talks about leaving the hole and going back up into the world which he has temporarily abandoned. You don't know how long the narrator has been in the hole, but you may infer that his main activity there has been writing the novel. When he has completed that, he will then rejoin the world of action. Thus, the Prologue and Epilogue frame the novel, putting it in the context of the narrator's present thoughts about life and activity. The narrator is finally not just the person to whom these events have occurred but the person who is organizing them into a work of art that tries to explain their significance. In the process, he creates himself.

The main body of the novel is a straightforward chronological narration of the protagonist's development. It may be divided into two, three, or four parts, depending on where you think the main structural breaks are. Ellison gives you only chapters, so the division into larger units is up to you. One structural principle is the movement from South to North (see comments under Setting). A second is that of death and rebirth. If you look at the death and rebirth structure, the novel would break into four major sections. Section I (Chapters 1 to 6) takes place in the South, mainly at the college. The narrator is expelled and this way of life is literally dead for him. In Section II (Chapters 7 to 12) he is born again in New York, only to have that existence literally exploded by the accident in the paint factory. Section III (Chapters 13 to 22) tells the story of his life with the Brotherhood and its eventual destruction. Section IV (Chapter 23 to the Epilogue) reveals the narrator's brief existence as Rinehart followed by his decision to disappear and rethink his values from his underground hole. He says at the end, using the words of the German philosopher Nietzsche, "I must shake off the old skin and come up for breath." Life is a series of rebirths, a process of shaking off the old skin (rind) over and over.

Whatever pattern you think is the most essential, the novel is fundamentally a developmental novel, a Bildungsroman in which a young man goes through a series of difficult and confusing experiences on the way to his maturity. Your main job is to discover what each of those experiences contributes to his growth.

The Story
PROLOGUE

You might think of the Prologue as a personal introduction. "I am an invisible man," is the first sentence of the novel. It establishes immediately the fact that this is to be a first-person narrative and that the theme of invisibility—which gives the novel its title—is extremely important. The nameless narrator explains that this invisibility is not literal but metaphorical or symbolic. He is invisible, he tells you, because people don't *see* him. They see only "my surroundings, themselves, or figments of their imagination." One reason for this is racial. The narrator is a black man, invisible because white people in America refuse to see black people as human beings, as individuals. He is also invisible because he has never developed his own identity but has instead played the roles that other people, especially white people, have required of him. But he doesn't really know that yet. It is something he will come to learn as he tells his life story.

The narrator is living in an abandoned cellar in a section of New York City bordering on Harlem, but it is not a dark cellar. It is lit by 1369 light bulbs, paid for by Monopolated Light & Power, which doesn't know where all that electricity is going. The narrator is fighting white power by draining off their electricity. It is also a warm cellar, a place where he can think and listen to music and try to figure out the meaning of his life up to this point. The narrator presents himself as a man in hiding who is preparing for a return to the real world, where he can take part in some action.

NOTE: Louis Armstrong, "What did I do/To be so black/And blue?"   Three times in the Prologue the narrator refers to the great black trumpet player and singer, Louis Armstrong, playing and singing this song, a recording of which is available. It is the first of many references to the blues, an important tradition in black music that allows both performer and listener to express their suffering in musical terms, to make art out of their pain and sorrow. Ellison himself writes in his essay, "Richard Wright's Blues," "The Blues is an impulse to keep the painful details and episodes of brutal experience alive in one's aching consciousness, to finger its jagged grain, and to transcend it, not by the consolation of philosophy, but by squeezing from it a near-tragic, near-comic lyricism." The title "Black and Blue" is a pun on both words. It means "bruised" or "hurt." It also means "a member of the black race" and "sad or depressed." Thus, when the narrator asks, in the last line of the Prologue, "What did *I* do to be so black and blue?", he is asking several questions at the same time. The story that begins in Chapter 1 is the narrator's attempt to answer those questions.

CHAPTER 1

Chapter 1, originally published before the rest of the novel as a short story called "Battle Royal," is the most famous chapter of the novel. It is often discussed by readers as a story complete in itself. You may enjoy reading it as a kind of parable about the general condition of black people in the South before the Civil Rights movement that began in the late 1950s.

The narrator is seventeen or eighteen. He has just graduated from high school in a southern town called Greenwood and has made a speech in the style of Booker T. Washington calling for blacks to be socially responsible and cooperative with whites. He has been invited, as the top-ranked black student, to give the speech again to a group of the leading white male citizens of the town at an evening "smoker" in the ballroom of the town's main hotel. What he does not know is that before he is allowed to give the speech, he must participate with nine other black boys in a "battle royal."

The ten black boys, supplied with shorts and boxing gloves, are herded like cattle into the ballroom, where they are forced to watch a blonde white woman do a provocative striptease, full of sexually arousing movements. The narrator is both attracted and repulsed by this woman. She is a symbol of everything the black man must confront

in America. He is made to want her, but told he
cannot have her, ordered to *watch* her, but punished should he show any signs of desiring her.
At the same time she is mauled and caressed by
drunken white men who can do what they want
and go unpunished because they have the power.

The whites are both sadistic and hypocritical.
They obviously enjoy watching the black boys suffer and seem to feel no guilt over their own behavior. After the girl is carried out, they blindfold
the ten black boys and force them into a ring where
they will blindly attack one another and get *paid*
by the whites for it. Many readers have noticed
that the "battle royal" is a prefiguration of the ending, where the blacks in Harlem riot, essentially
hurting one another, while the whites stand by
and watch.

NOTE: Blindness as symbol   Throughout the novel
the contrast between sight and blindness will play
a major role. In this scene the symbol of blindness
is introduced through the imaginative use of the
blindfolds. Reread the battle royal scene and look
for the various ways in which the inability to see
outwardly parallels the inability to understand in-
wardly. The narrator is able to avoid being hurt
when he can peep through his blindfold. One of
the boys breaks his hand because he hits the ring
post. The fight is sheer anarchy, because blindness
reduces the black boys to nothing more than flail-
ing beasts. How can blacks expect to gain dignity
when they are figuratively "blindfolded" by whites?

After a period of time, the blindfolds are removed and the narrator finds himself alone in the ring with a big black named Tatlock. They are expected to box for the championship. At first the narrator does well, but when he hears one of the powerful whites say, "I got my money on the big boy," he stops trying, because he is afraid that he might offend the whites by winning and thus not be asked to make his speech. As a result, he is knocked out.

But his humiliation is not over. When he recovers, the other boys are brought back in, and all of them are told to get their money from a rug covered with coins, bills, and gold pieces. They scramble for the money, only to be violently shocked. The rug has been electrified. This scene is not only horrifying in itself, but as some readers have noticed, it foreshadows the scene in Chapter 11 when the narrator is given electric shock therapy in the factory hospital, again by white people, who find it interesting to "experiment" on blacks.

Before he is allowed to receive the award for achievement, the young narrator is forced to undergo one more humiliation. He must give the speech, his mouth filled with blood and saliva, to an audience of drunks who either mock or ignore him. He is forced to repeat the phrase "social responsibility," and at one point he mistakenly says "social equality." There is a sudden stillness in the room; the boy corrects himself, and everything is all right. But the point of the lesson is clear. Blacks are to rise, but always and only by the rules whites make.

To encourage him along these lines, the white leaders present him with a calfskin briefcase, in which he finds a document announcing his scholarship to the "state college for Negroes." Both of these props are important in the subsequent development of the novel. The briefcase follows the narrator through all his adventures and remains in the hole with him at the end. Most of the narrator's significant possessions wind up in that briefcase. The scholarship, of course, is the first item in the briefcase. More importantly, it is the first of three crucial pieces of paper given to the narrator by white groups. Each of these pieces of paper serves to identify him, name him for a portion of the novel.

The meaning of these documents is suggested in a dream the narrator has at the end of the chapter. He dreams he is at the circus with his strange grandfather and that he is asked to open his briefcase. In it is a letter, and in that another letter, and so endlessly until a final document engraved in gold contains the words: "To Whom It May Concern, Keep This Nigger-Boy Running." At the time the narrator is too young and too naive to understand the meaning of the dream. What is your interpretation?

CHAPTER 2

Three years have passed. The narrator is now a junior at the state college for blacks. He is doing very well and has been such a model student that he is entrusted with the job of chauffeuring important guests around the campus and its surroundings.

NOTE: The college and Eliot's *The Waste Land*
Before the action of Chapter 2 begins, the narrator describes the college in terms borrowed directly from T. S. Eliot's *The Waste Land.* We know that

Ellison read the poem during his years at Tuskegee
Institute (the model for the college in the novel),
and in this section he implies that the college was
a kind of waste land by using Eliot's language.
"Why does no rain fall through my recollections?"
the narrator asks, paralleling the narrator's thoughts
of dryness in Eliot. And the phrase "Oh, oh, oh
those multimillionaires" is borrowed from Eliot's
"O O O O that Shakespeherian Rag." When you
get deeper into the book, you will be better able
to understand why the narrator views the college
as a waste land. What clues do you have at this
point?

The chapter opens on Founder's Day, the day
set aside each spring to honor the mythical founder
of the college. Many of the distinguished white
multimillionaires who serve as trustees are present
for the occasion. The narrator has been engaged
to drive one of them, a Mr. Norton. Since there is
plenty of time before Mr. Norton's next engage-
ment, they drive into the country and end up at
the run-down farm of a black sharecropper named
Jim Trueblood. Mr. Norton wants to find out the
age and history of the place, but the narrator is
uncomfortable at the thought of stopping. Trueblood had created a scandal by having fathered a
child of his own daughter, and the narrator knows
the school officials will be furious if they discover
that Mr. Norton has been to see Trueblood. But
Norton is fascinated, and the more the narrator
tells him about Trueblood, the more Norton wants
to talk with him. We begin to understand Norton's
interest in Trueblood when we remember the white
man's conversation with the narrator at the start

of the chapter. Norton had been telling the narrator about his only daughter, whom he loved more than anything else in the world. He and his daughter had been traveling in Europe when she died. Norton's gifts to the black college have all been in her memory. Did Norton feel an incestuous attraction to his daughter? Is he fascinated by Trueblood because Trueblood *did* what he, Norton, wanted (in his blood) to do but was terrified of doing? You will have to decide what you think here, but many readers have found the parallels between Norton and Trueblood intriguing and important.

Norton persuades Trueblood to tell his story. What Trueblood has to say is important not only for what he reveals but also for how he tells it. Trueblood is the first of several important Afro-American folk figures that Ellison creates. He is a storyteller, a singer of spirituals, and a blues singer. He tells Norton, ". . . while I'm singin' them blues I makes up my mind that I ain't nobody but myself and ain't nothin' I can do but let whatever is gonna happen, happen." This is a lesson that it will take the narrator the entire novel to learn.

Trueblood doesn't think it out before he commits incest with his daughter. He doesn't plan it. Perhaps his name "True" combined with "blood" suggests his character. He is true to himself and he follows his blood. The incest takes place almost in a dream where he can feel his body doing it without his mind really knowing that it is happening. Afterwards his wife Kate nearly kills him with an axe, but he decides to stay with his wife and daughter and *both* their children. He will live the best he can, no matter what people say. The blacks at the college hate him (and, of course, the narrator is one of them) because they see him as the sort of black man they are trying *not* to be. But white people are fascinated by Trueblood. They give him money and come to hear his story, and so he ends up much better off than he was before the incident. Norton, too, gives Trueblood $100 after hearing the story, and the narrator is furious. "You no good bastard!" he says under his breath, not wanting to offend the white man, and the scene is complete.

CHAPTER 3

The shock of Trueblood's story has made Mr. Norton feel faint, and he asks the narrator to get him some whiskey. The only place the narrator can think to take him is the Golden Day, a wild combination of tavern and house of prostitution that is—like Trueblood's place—off limits to the college students. It is a world that the leaders at the college pretend does not exist. Just as the narrator pulls up to the Golden Day, a group of black war veterans from the local state hospital are on their way to the place for their weekly recreation. They have all been affected mentally by their war experience and exhibit a variety of bizarre symptoms. They allow the narrator's car to pass when he tells them he is driving General Pershing, their commander in the war.

The narrator doesn't want Mr. Norton to see the patients or the girls; so he asks the bartender to let him take the whiskey to the car. The bartender refuses, and there is no way to revive Norton, who has by now passed out, except to carry him into the Golden Day and pour the whiskey down his throat. Norton revives, but at this moment a huge black named Supercargo, who is the attendant, appears on the balcony. The vets hate him and charge the stairs. A riot breaks out, and in the process the narrator loses Mr. Norton. Finally, he finds him, passed out again, under the stairs. This time some of the vets carry Norton upstairs to one of the prostitute's rooms where he is again revived and cared for by a whore named Edna and a patient named Burnside, who was a doctor before the war.

NOTE: Burnside The fat veteran-patient who takes care of Mr. Norton in this chapter makes a brief but significant appearance (you see him only once more, in Chapter 7, on the bus to New York). He is the first black man who talks openly to a white man, and that fact scares the narrator, who is too intimidated by whites to realize that they are just human beings, too. Burnside is a doctor, and he not only knows that Norton needs help ("He's only a man. Remember that."), but he knows that the narrator is "a walking zombie! Already he's learned to repress not only his emotions but his humanity." Burnside tries to teach the narrator a lesson about life, but the narrator is too rigid, too narrow-minded at this point in his life to get the message. So is Mr. Norton. They both see the important work of black-white relations as somehow tied to the college. Burnside, especially, and the other vets at the Golden Day are trying to say that the work must be done in the real world. Since Trueblood and Burnside are an important part of the narrator's education, why does he reject them at this point in his life?

The chapter ends with the narrator and Mr. Norton being literally thrown out the door of the Golden Day. Mr. Norton, who it seemed was nearly dead, makes a strong recovery and walks to the car unaided. "DEAD!" says the bartender, Halley. "He *cain't* die!" The statement, like so many others, has multiple meanings, one of which is that the white money that Norton represents is *always* there. It can't be killed. Can you think of other interpretations of this passage?

CHAPTER 4

The narrator, full of fear, drives Mr. Norton back to the campus. The life he has found for himself at the college means everything to him. His goal is to imitate Mr. Bledsoe, the president, by becoming an educator, by returning to teach at the college after he has completed his own training. He hates Jim Trueblood and the vets at the Golden Day for ruining his life, because all he can see now is that he will surely be dismissed for what has happened to Mr. Norton. And yet, somehow, it does not seem to be his fault. It just happened!

But whether it is his fault or not, he must face the consequences in the person of the furious Dr. Bledsoe. He lashes out at the narrator in language that the narrator has never heard before. "Damn what *he* wants," says Bledsoe about Mr. Norton, "we take these white folks where we want them to go, we show them what we want them to see." The narrator cannot believe he is hearing such talk from Dr. Bledsoe, who has always been so humble and dignified and apparently obedient to the wishes of white people. In front of Mr. Norton, Bledsoe returns to the role of the polite but humble black educator; alone with the narrator he is blunt and brutal, but the narrator is too naive to grasp what is going on.

He returns to his room and tries to puzzle out Bledsoe's behavior, but before he can, a message sends him back to Mr. Norton's room at Rabb Hall. Mr. Norton is a different person now. Bathed and dressed in fresh clothes, he is the distant northern trustee you might have expected to meet earlier. He is civil but cool toward the narrator and informs him that he is leaving the college that evening and will no longer require the narrator's services. He sends the boy out the door, reminding him that he is to see Dr. Bledsoe in his office after vespers.

CHAPTER 5

Chapter 5 consists almost entirely of a long, brilliantly written sermon delivered by Reverend Homer A. Barbee of Chicago. The occasion for the sermon is Founder's Day, and the purpose of the sermon is to honor the unnamed founder of the college, a man whose life and work Barbee transforms into a myth, almost a religion.

NOTE: The "Founder" and Booker T. Washington The college in the novel is modeled in part on Tuskegee Institute, which Ellison attended from 1933 to 1936. The great black leader Booker T. Washington (1856–1915) founded Tuskegee in 1881 and ran it on the fundamental principles of "separate but equal," which became both custom and law in the South during the 1890s. Washington encouraged blacks to learn useful trades and not to aspire to equality with whites. He was an astute fund raiser and a politically adept leader who succeeded in building Tuskegee into a major national force in black education. You may wish to explore the extent to which the founder in the novel is modeled on Washington.

As the narrator waits for the sermon to begin, he thinks of the many hours he has sat on those hard benches and listened to the choir sing songs demanded by the distinguished white visitors. He thinks of the times he has spoken and debated as a student leader, and he watches Dr. Bledsoe, distinguished in his swallowtail coat and striped trousers, seating the white guests on the platform.

At this point you must read very carefully. Ellison uses a technique that recurs throughout the novel. He lets the narrator tell you something with a straight face, but invites you to see the humor or the irony that the narrator misses. Speaking of Bledsoe's arrival at the college as a child, he tells us: "I remember the legend of how he had come to the college, a barefoot boy who in his fervor for education had trudged across two states. And how he was given a job feeding slop to the hogs but had made himself the best slop dispenser in the history of the school. . . ." From slop dispenser he rises to office boy and from office boy to educator, from educator to president, from president to statesman, "who carried our problems to those above us, even unto the White House."

How are you to take this story? Or the story of the Founder, told by the black minister, Homer A. Barbee, which makes the Founder seem like a combination of Moses and Jesus Christ? In both cases, the stories are obviously exaggerated. The myths of Bledsoe and the Founder endow these men with almost superhuman qualities. If you can understand *why*, then you can enjoy what Ellison is doing and what the narrator misses. It *suits* the college to mythologize Bledsoe's past. It *suits* Homer A. Barbee to make the Founder into a religious figure worthy of worship, because these legends and myths create loyalty in their followers. These legends keep the white philanthropists giving money and keep the students following their teachings. When the narrator hears Barbee's beautiful story of the life of the Founder, born a slave but devoted from his early childhood to learning, he feels guilty that he has wronged the college by his mistakes, and he believes that *he*, not Bledsoe, is the one who has acted improperly.

All the students are moved by the sermon, and they join in song, this time one sincerely felt. The narrator feels confused and apart, and when the orchestra plays excerpts from Antonín Dvořák's symphony *From the New World* he keeps hearing strains of his mother and his grandfather's favorite spiritual, "Swing Low, Sweet Chariot." Too moved to listen, he leaves the chapel and hurries out into the dark.

NOTE: Homer A. Barbee Ellison enjoys using symbols. At the end of Homer A. Barbee's speech, he stumbles and falls, his dark glasses drop to the floor, and the narrator realizes that the man is blind. The combination of his name and blindness suggest his role. He is Homer, the blind Greek bard (bard = barbee?), who sings the praises of his heroes, Bledsoe and the Founder, as Homer sang the praises of the Greek and Trojan warriors on the plains of Troy.

CHAPTER 6

The moment the narrator has been dreading arrives: the confrontation with Bledsoe. Mostly dialogue, this would be a powerful scene to read aloud with a friend or to act out in front of a class. Bledsoe tears into the narrator for taking Norton to Trueblood's and the Golden Day. He accuses the boy of dragging the name of the college into the mud, and he expels him. But the narrator doesn't take it lying down. He fights back, calling Bledsoe a liar for going back on his word to Mr. Norton that he would not punish him. Bledsoe shocks the boy by suddenly changing tactics. He admires the boy's fight, and he levels with him for a moment. "I'm still the king down here," he tells the narrator, "and I will do whatever I have to do to keep my power. I'll have every Negro in the country hanging on tree limbs by morning if it means staying where I am."

Like an expert boxer, he shoots jabs and hooks at the narrator's weak defenses, reducing him to helplessness. You begin to see the implications of Bledsoe's name—he "bleeds his people so" in order to secure and advance his own power. He works with the whites because it suits him. This is too much for the narrator to handle. He thinks of all the events of this one day—Trueblood, Mr. Norton, the Golden Day, the vespers sermon, and now Bledsoe's confession. What does it all mean? He thinks of his grandfather, who had told him on his deathbed (at the outset of Chapter 1) "to overcome 'em with yeses, undermine 'em with grins, agree 'em to death and destruction.'' For a moment he wonders if his grandfather's advice has not been right. But he cannot let himself believe that his true role in life ought to be the undermining of white society. No, the school is right, Bledsoe is right, he thinks. He decides to accept his punishment, go to New York, and continue to build his "career" from there.

The next morning he rises early, packs his bags, and goes to Bledsoe's office to ask a favor: He would like letters of recommendation to some of the trustees, who then might help him find a job. With the job he will be able to earn the money to come back to school. He will suffer his punishment and return. Bledsoe seemingly agrees and gives the boy seven sealed letters. He is not to open them under any circumstances.

CHAPTER 7

Chapter 7 is a transitional chapter between two major sections of *Invisible Man.* Ellison does not divide the novel into formal parts or books, so you must make the divisions yourself. Many readers place a major break here in Chapter 7, following Ellison's own suggestion. In "The Art of Fiction: An Interview," Ellison says, "Each section begins with a sheet of paper; each sheet of paper is exchanged for another and contains a definition of his identity, or the social role he is to play as defined for him by others." (See The Critics section for the entire passage.)

The first piece of paper referred to seems to be the scholarship given him in Chapter 1. The second piece of paper may well be the letters given to him by Bledsoe at the end of Chapter 6. These letters will define his identity in New York in Chapters 7 to 9. But first he has to get there, and much of Chapter 7 is taken up with the bus trip to New York, where he meets again the vet-patient-doctor from Chapter 3, Burnside. Burnside is being transferred to St. Elizabeth's mental hospital in Washington and is being accompanied on the trip by an attendant named Crenshaw.

Burnside, as he did in Chapter 3, plays the role of the wise fool. He knows the truth, and for his knowledge he is called crazy. Bledsoe, it seems, has had him transferred to St. Elizabeth's to get him out of the way. For those who run the system, people like Burnside are dangerous, because they threaten to expose the truth. During the bus ride, Burnside gives the narrator some good advice about life, experience and self-knowledge. He tells him to play the game, but "play it in your own way. . . . Learn how it operates."

The narrator seems to understand little of what Burnside is saying. He is too young, too tired, too lonely, and too scared. At this moment all he can think of is survival. He gets to New York and is terrified by the mass of bodies crushed together in the subway that takes him uptown. Everything is new to him—the huge city with its impersonal masses, the mixture of black and white he had never seen in the South, the noise, the strange sight of a short black rabble-rouser named "Ras," who will much later in the novel figure very significantly. He has arrived in Harlem.

CHAPTER 8

The narrator settles in at Men's House in Harlem, a respectable place for young men "on the way up,'' as he believes himself to be. He rejects the Bible in the room as fit reading for someone in New York; instead, he spreads his seven letters from Bledsoe on the dresser and admires them. He believes they are his ticket to success, and he starts out early the next morning to deliver them, one at a time, to the important people to whom they are addressed. Most of these people work on Wall Street, and at first the narrator is frightened of the tall buildings and the swiftly moving crowds of white businessmen. He thinks people suspect him of some crime because he is black. But he finally gathers the courage to go into one of the buildings, and after he has delivered the first letter, delivering the others is easier. But the letters do not seem to do any good. All the recipients say they will contact him, but no one does. He tries to reach them by telephone, but he can never get past the secretaries. Something is wrong, but he doesn't know what it is.

Finally, he has only one letter left, the one addressed to Mr. Emerson, and rather than taking the letter and risking rejection, he telephones, saying that he has an important message for Mr. Emerson from Dr. Bledsoe. Just as his money is about to run out, he receives a letter from Mr. Emerson inviting him to the office.

CHAPTER 9

Chapter 8, a brief chapter, was largely devoted to forwarding the action. Chapter 9 is more central to the themes of the novel. In it you are introduced to two important figures: Peter Wheatstraw and young Mr. Emerson. As the narrator leaves Men's House, he sees a black man pushing a cart and singing the famous "Boogie Woogie Blues" by Count Basie and Jimmy Rushing. His name is Peter Wheatstraw, and he does something significant: He makes the narrator think of his southern folk roots. He recognizes the narrator as a fellow black from "down home," and he asks him a series of questions, using language common among less educated southern blacks. He does so deliberately to remind the narrator that he is part of that folk tradition. The narrator rejects him. He's too proud, too educated to acknowledge an illiterate southern black like Peter Wheatstraw. "Why you trying to deny me?" Wheatstraw asks. The question is important. The narrator has been trying since the opening chapter to deny his heritage, to act like an educated white man. He is ashamed of himself and his heritage. He can see no value in it. Peter Wheatstraw, the blues singer, ballad maker, fast-talking "seventhsonofaseventhsonbawnwithacaul-overbotheyes," is there to remind the narrator that rejecting the blues and folk tradition means rejecting his humanity.

But the narrator isn't ready yet to get the message. He has a momentary flash of admiration for Peter, and the blues strike a chord of recognition. But it passes, and he goes into a restaurant and orders orange juice, toast, and coffee instead of pork chops, grits, one egg, biscuits, and coffee because he doesn't want the people to think he is a southern country boy.

After breakfast he goes to Mr. Emerson's office, hopeful it will be his lucky day. What happens to him here is one of the major turning points in the novel. Young Mr. Emerson, the son of the Emerson to whom the letter was addressed, is in the office. He takes the letter, then invites the invisible man into the inner office. There follows a remarkable conversation that lasts for eight or ten pages. Mr. Emerson tries to persuade the narrator to go to a different college, somewhere in the North, perhaps. But the narrator is not interested. He wants to earn the money to go back to his own college. Mr. Emerson grows increasingly disturbed. He asks more questions. Has the narrator opened the letters? How many letters were there? Does he believe that two strangers, one white and one black, can be friends? The narrator wonders what is going on, and you are as puzzled as he unless you have figured the truth out first. Perhaps you have. The truth is that the letters are frauds: the letters, rather than helping the narrator, carefully instruct their readers to do nothing for the narrator and to keep him in the dark about the truth. All this, the letters conclude, is in the best interests of the college. You now understand the significance of the narrator's dream at the end of Chapter 1, where he opens the envelope and reads the message: "To Whom It May Concern—Keep This Nigger-Boy Running." For that is exactly what Bledsoe's letters instruct the white trustees to do. And the narrator never suspected it. Again, the narrator has lost his identity. The letters were all he had, and he remembers the old folk song, "Well they picked poor Robin clean." It seems especially appropriate for him at this moment.

But young Mr. Emerson is not old Mr. Emerson. He is not content with reading the letter and dismissing the boy. As we have noted in The Characters section, he may represent the young, liberal white who wants to be "pals" with the black man. He thinks of himself as Huckleberry Finn and the narrator as "Nigger Jim." He wants to work off his own guilt by taking the narrator to nightclubs and listening to jazz. He wants to be cool and modern and go to the Club Calamus (see The Characters for an analysis of the name). At the end of the chapter he honestly believes that his revelation of the truth about the letters has genuinely helped the narrator. But has it?

NOTE: The name "Emerson"   Ralph Waldo Emerson (1803–1882) was the most influential writer in America during the first half of the nineteenth century. His essays "Nature," "The American Scholar," and "Self Reliance" urged Americans, young Americans particularly, to think for themselves and base their ideas on personal intuition rather than convention. He was also an active supporter of the abolition of slavery and a believer in the equality of all men. As noted in The Author and His Times, Ellison was named for Emerson, and he appreciated the significance of the name. Why, then, you might ask, is the central figure in this chapter named Emerson? The issue has been discussed in the The Characters section, and you might find it useful to review that section now in the context of Chapter 9.

At the end of the chapter the narrator is furious. He leaves the office and returns to Men's House with "they picked poor Robin clean" on his brain. He swears revenge on Bledsoe. But before he can kill Bledsoe, he has to have a job. So he takes a job at the Liberty Paint Factory, the place Mr. Emerson has sent a number of young men before. The juxtaposition of the projected murder and the job is wonderfully ironic, and allows you to see, once more, the difference between the hero's real character and his perception of himself. Poor Robin!

CHAPTER 10

If you are the adventuresome type, you will have a field day with Chapter 10. It's one of the liveliest, most imaginative chapters in the novel. Because it is symbolic, it will challenge you from beginning to end to use your mind while you are reading.

The narrator arrives at the plant on Long Island and sees a huge electric sign announcing KEEP AMERICA PURE WITH LIBERTY PAINTS. As he enters one of the buildings and walks down a "pure white hall," you are alerted to the fact that the plant is going to be a symbol for white America. The company's trademark is "a screaming eagle," and they specialize in white paint, *pure* white paint, which they sell to the government. Apparently the Liberty Paint Company uses a number of "colored college boys" so that they don't have to pay union wages. But the black workers are well hidden.

The narrator is sent by Mr. MacDuffy to work for a Mr. Kimbro, the terrible Mr. Kimbro (who is called "Colonel"—perhaps suggesting the tyranny of the colonels of the Old South over blacks) in the paint-testing department. Kimbro's job is to inspect the paint before it is loaded, and he shows the narrator how to assist him. The paint looks brown on the surface, before it is mixed, but after it is stirred, the brown disappears and the paint turns white. But Kimbro is not satisfied. The paint isn't white enough, and so he directs the narrator to put ten drops of *black* coloring into each bucket to make it a purer white—"Optic White," which is the company's specialty. It doesn't make much sense to the narrator to use black coloring to make paint white, but Kimbro says, "You just do what you're told and don't try to think about it."

Kimbro has to go to a production conference, and the narrator runs out of coloring. So he goes to the tank room to get more but finds that there are two tanks that look exactly alike. He picks the tank that smells most like the coloring, refills his bucket, and completes the job. When Kimbro comes back, he is furious. The narrator, by thinking for himself, has picked the wrong tank and used concentrated remover instead. Kimbro has him put the proper coloring into the cans with the remover and seems satisfied that the problem has been solved, even though the narrator thinks the paint looks a little gray.

How do you interpret the symbolism of this little story? If the black coloring stands for black people, then how are black people used to make white America work? "Optic White" means white in appearance, or to the eye, as in optical illusion. The white paint is not *really* white, as America is not really white, but it requires blacks behind the scenes in cooperation with whites to make the white world work. What kinds of blacks does white America need to have in order to keep up this facade? Perhaps Mr. Kimbro's treatment of the narrator suggests the answer.

NOTE: Expressionism   In the section on "Style" Ellison was quoted as saying that the style of the novel was at first realistic, but that it became expressionistic after the narrator moved North. Chapters 10 and 11 are perhaps the best examples of Ellison's expressionism (review the Style section for a definition). Chapters 10 and 11 are hard to believe literally. If you read them as realistic pictures of life in a paint factory, you will be disappointed. What Ellison is doing here is trying to depict expressionistically what white America is doing to blacks for its own selfish ends. The real action of these chapters is *inner*, not *outer*.

In the second half of Chapter 10, the scene shifts to the basement of Building No. 2. Kimbro has sent the narrator here, because he doesn't want anyone who thinks for himself working for him. Thinking creates trouble! The narrator's boss in the basement is an old black man named Lucius Brockway. Brockway makes the *guts* of the paint down in this deep basement. Again, note the symbolism. Deep underground a black man makes the guts of the white paint that keeps this white factory going. Not only does he make it, he is the one who coined the slogan, "If It's Optic White, It's the Right White." The narrator realizes that this is just another way of saying, "If you're white, you're right."

If you are enjoying the fun of Ellison's complex symbolism, you have probably figured out that Lucius Brockway is like the ten drops of black coloring the narrator had to pour in the bucket to make Optic White look white. Without the black man in the basement doing the dirty work, the whites would be lost. No one knows how to make the paint except Lucius. If he retired, the place would collapse. And he likes it. He is the perfect Uncle Tom. He sacrifices himself (he keeps out of sight) to keep the whites white.

The narrator and Lucius get along well until the narrator stumbles across a union meeting on his way to get his lunch out of his locker. The union people think he is a fink, a hired strike breaker, because he works for Lucius, whom they hate. Then, when the narrator returns, Lucius calls him a louse for attending the union meeting. The Invisible Man can't win.

The narrator may be naive, but he is a fighter. Just as he argued with Bledsoe and young Mr. Emerson, he holds his own with Lucius Brockway, and because he is younger and physically stronger, he can force Brockway to back down. Brockway finally admits that he doesn't like the union because it is critical of the white bosses. The union threatens the relationship between white power and black Uncle Toms. But just as the narrator thinks that peace has been restored, Brockway notices that the pressure gauge his new assistant is supposed to have been watching has gone way up. The narrator has literally "blown it" again. There is a huge explosion, and the narrator is knocked unconscious into a "blast of black emptiness that was somehow a bath of whiteness." The symbolism of the chapter is complete. The black man is immersed in a world of white.

CHAPTER 11

If the primary symbolism of Chapter 10 is black vs white, then Chapter 11 operates around the symbolism of death and rebirth. In this chapter the narrator, who has been symbolically killed in Chapter 10, is resurrected with a new identity.

The action takes place in the factory hospital,

where the narrator has been taken after the explosion. He is examined and then subjected to electric shock treatment. After the electric shock, he wakes to find himself lying in "a kind of glass and nickel box." He is being used for some sort of experiment. He hears men talking outside the box. One is a surgeon who would like to do a prefrontal lobotomy on him, or perhaps, castration. The surgeon wants to cut out of the black man anything that would allow him to be thoughtful or creative, in any sense.

The other man is the inventor of the machine in which the narrator finds himself. The man believes that his machine—with its electric shock—will have all the positive effects of the surgery (making the black man docile and cooperative) without the negative effects. The two argue over the narrator as if he were some kind of object, finally deciding to use the machine. After another series of shocks, the narrator feels himself in a warm, watery world. It is as if he is an infant being born.

He emerges from the womb, and people begin to ask him questions. WHAT IS YOUR NAME? WHAT IS YOUR MOTHER'S NAME? WHO WAS BUCKEYE THE RABBIT?

NOTE: Buckeye the Rabbit In Afro-American folklore, Buckeye the Rabbit is the same as Brer Rabbit. Both had the reputation in a variety of tales of being able to escape from the most difficult predicaments by their cleverness and toughness. The most famous of these tales is the story of the Tar Baby, to which Ellison refers more than once in the novel. Perhaps the narrator, like Brer Rabbit, escapes from the machine because he remembers these stories from his childhood and they help give him a toughness, an identity of sorts, at a time when the whites are trying to destroy it altogether. Because he says nothing to them, they don't know what he is thinking.

As the chapter ends, the narrator is released from the hospital, having been pronounced "cured." The whites believe that he is "safe" now, that he will not do any more harm, because he has lost his old identity entirely. They get him to sign some release papers, and they will pay him compensation in return for a promise not to hold them responsible. He leaves the hospital, remembering the song he sang at the end of Chapter 9: "They picked poor Robin clean."

CHAPTER 12

Chapter 12 is a transitional chapter, marking the end of the first half of the novel and the beginning of the second. The narrator emerges from the subway onto Lenox Avenue in Harlem feeling like an infant. Totally helpless after his experience in the hospital, he needs someone to care for him, and that someone appears in the person of Mary Rambo (see The Characters).

The narrator is a child who needs a mother, and Mary—big bosomed, deep-voiced, patient, and loving—has been created for the role. She takes him to her boarding house, puts him to bed, and watches over him until he is strong enough to go back to Men's House. She invites him to come back and stay, where she can care for him and keep him from becoming corrupted by New York.

He returns to Men's House, but he is not the same man who left it: "My overalls were causing stares and I knew that I could live there no longer, that that phase of my life was past." He can no longer dream of moving up in the white man's world. And because he no longer has that dream, his vision of Men's House changes. He (in his painter's overalls) sees the young men with their Brooks Brothers suits and briefcases and umbrellas as a bunch of phonies. As he starts toward the elevator he sees a figure in front of him whom he immediately believes to be Bledsoe. In his mind he calls him "Bled," appropriate for the man who has "bled" him so. Suddenly all the hate and frustration in him rises, and he picks up a brass spittoon full of "brown liquid" and dumps it over the man's head. But it is not Bledsoe! Instead, it is a well-known Baptist minister, and the narrator is forced to run for cover. This is the last he sees of Men's House; they have barred him for "ninety-nine years and a day."

His old identity is gone, and a new one has started to grow within him. He returns to Mary's as a child returns to its parent. She nurtures him, but she also pushes him, as a mother, to grow up and do something responsible. He senses that she is right, but he doesn't know what to do. He has no contacts, no job, no direction. His compensation money is running out, and winter is coming on. His head is full of voices, full of the desire to speak out (but about what he doesn't know). He tries to face the reality of his condition for the first time. The invisible man is on the verge of discovering a new self, another identity.

CHAPTER 13

Chapter 13 is the central chapter of the novel. In a novel with 25 chapters, a Prologue, and an Epilogue, it is near the exact middle. That is no accident, for in this chapter the narrator undergoes the most important event in his life thus far: He finds a calling as a spokesman for his people. There are three important events in the chapter: (1) the episode with the yam seller, (2) the narrator's speech at the eviction, and (3) his first conversation with the dominant figure of the second half of the novel, Brother Jack.

As the chapter opens, the narrator is profoundly unsettled. He has no job, no money, no identity. As he rushes out of the house into the street, he runs into the yam seller, an old man "wrapped in an army overcoat, his feet covered with gunny sacks, his head in a knitted cap. . . ." Had the narrator run into the yam seller even as much as two or three chapters earlier, he would have avoided him as the very type of black man he most disapproved of—an old country black, uneducated, crude, and poor. But something in the factory experience has changed the narrator, and the yams remind him of home, of his family and childhood. He is hungry—both literally and figuratively—for the hot yams, bubbling with butter and syrup. He buys one and eats it, right there on the street. All at once he has what James Joyce called an "epiphany"—a sudden moment of illumination, of insight into himself. He says, "It was exhilarating. I no longer had to worry about who saw me or about what was proper . . . to hell with being ashamed of what you liked. No more of that for me."

He buys two yams and eats them on the street for all to see. He feels a new sense of freedom, and he announces, "I yam what I am."

He suddenly thinks of proper Dr. Bledsoe, that model of propriety, eating chitterlings secretly in private so white men won't see him. He laughs and accuses Bledsoe of being a secret chitterling eater, of "relishing hog bowels." He will expose Bledsoe as a fraud.

NOTE: Chitterlings   Sometimes called "chitlins" or "chittlings," chitterlings are the cooked small intestines of hogs. In this section, Ellison has the narrator mention not only chitterlings, but also pigs' ears, pork chops, black-eyed peas, and mustard greens. All these are foods commonly eaten by southern blacks. Bledsoe and the narrator have been trying to deny both their blackness and their southern heritage. They have denied their fundamental roots in black folk culture. The narrator suddenly realizes that he really *likes* these foods, but that he has stopped eating them because he is afraid of what others will think.

Armed with this new understanding about himself, that I am what I am, I am what I like, I can choose what I want to do on the basis of personal preference, the narrator feels both free and frightened. This new ability to be one's self implies the making of personal choices. He has never done that. He always did what others expected of him. As he thinks about this, he comes upon a scene in the street. An old black couple is being evicted from their apartment. All their personal belong-ings and furniture are being piled in the street by white marshals. A crowd has gathered, sullen, an-gry, resentful at what is being done.

The narrator has never seen an eviction. His eyes are opened for the first time to the reality of black life in America. He has always worked *for* whites. Now he begins *seeing*, both literally and figura-tively. He sees the couple's possessions on the street, and he understands the meaning of these possessions. It is as if his own grandparents are being evicted. He feels a sense of emotional iden-tification with these old people. They are *his people*. "It is as though I myself was being dispossessed of some painful yet precious thing which I could not bear to lose. . . ."

The old woman, Mrs. Provo, tries to go back into the house to pray one last time, but the marshals refuse to let her. One of them strikes her, and sud-denly the mob becomes angry. Then almost with-out warning the narrator becomes a leader. He fears the violence of the crowd and of himself, and he starts speaking to the group, trying to move the people to constructive action instead of useless violence. All the speeches he made in school and college seem to have prepared him for this mo-ment. The words come pouring out. He plays on the theme of dispossession, saying that all blacks are dispossessed, and he tries to persuade the mar-shals to let them all go in and pray. The crowd, moved by his speech, rushes past the marshals into the house, punching and beating them as they go. The narrator himself is caught up in the emo-tion of the scene. "Let's go in and pray," he shouts, "But we'll need some chairs." From chairs it is just a step to everything else, and the crowd excitedly starts carrying all the articles from the street back into the house.

At this point the narrator notices two white people, a man and a woman, who don't seem to be marshals. They act friendly, but not like anyone the narrator has ever seen before. They encourage the people to have a protest march, but before anything can be organized, the police come and break up the scene. The white woman tells the narrator to escape across the roofs of the buildings. "The longer you remain unknown to the police, the longer you'll be effective," she says. The narrator doesn't understand what she's saying, but he does what she suggests. He takes off across the roofs, followed by the white man who seems to be chasing him. He outdistances the man, goes down the stairs of another building at the end of the block, and walks out into the street. The police are nowhere to be seen, but he has not lost the man, who comes up to him and says, "That was a masterful bit of persuasion, brother."

The man takes the narrator to a cafeteria, buys him coffee and cheesecake (which the narrator has never tasted), and explains who he is. His name is Brother Jack and he works for an organization known as the Brotherhood. He is impressed with the narrator's speaking ability and wants him to join the organization and become a spokesman in Harlem, "someone who can articulate the grievances of the people." The narrator is hesitant. What is this organization? What do they want with him? Are they just interested in *using* him like everyone else? He thinks about it, then turns Brother Jack down, but he takes his phone number in case he changes his mind. Another important piece of paper!

NOTE: The Brotherhood and the Communist Party
Much has been written by a variety of critics about the relationship between the Brotherhood and the Communist party. Ellison himself comments on it in his "Art of Fiction" interview, and the American scholar and social critic Irving Howe (see The Critics) discusses it in some detail. This study guide comments on Ellison's relation to the Communists in the The Author and His Times section. While Ellison did not intend the Brotherhood to represent *only* the Communist party, he never denied that the parallel was valid. The Brotherhood may represent any organization that uses individuals and/or minority groups to enhance its own cause. We will explore this topic further as we go along.

CHAPTER 14

The narrator returns to Mary's and smells cabbage cooking. Since it's the third time this week Mary has cooked cabbage, the narrator assumes rightly that Mary must be short of money. He stops to think about Brother Jack's offer. Maybe he has made a mistake. How can he turn down a job when Mary needs the money and he is several months behind in his rent payments? Quickly he changes his mind and calls Brother Jack, who tells him to go to an address on Lenox Avenue. Here the narrator is picked up and whisked off through Central Park downtown to "an expensive-looking building in a strange part of the city." The building is called the Chthonian.

NOTE: Chthonian   In Greek mythology this is the name for the realm of the underworld, the realm of the dead. Why has Ellison chosen this name for the building in which the Brotherhood has its meetings? Is the narrator, in some sense, descending into the underworld by joining the Brotherhood? There is an eerie feeling in the building, with its "lobby lighted by dim bulbs" and its elevator that moves in such a way that the narrator is "uncertain whether we had gone up or down." Ellison, as always, is having fun with his symbols.

Brother Jack leads the narrator into an apartment in which a party is going on. The hostess at the party is a woman named Emma, who looks at the narrator in a way quite different from women in the South, a way that makes him uncomfortable. He is taken into the library for a meeting. Point blank he is asked if he would like to be the new Booker T. Washington.

NOTE: Booker T. Washington   Booker T. Washington's name is mentioned several times in this chapter. In an earlier note during the discussion of Chapter 5, the parallels between Booker T. Washington and the Founder were discussed. In this chapter, Ellison seems to contradict himself by having the narrator contrast the Founder with Booker T. Washington, treating them as two totally distinct people. You may find this confusing. The author appears to be using Booker T. Washington here for a different purpose than he did in Chapter 5. If you remember that Washington was the *white* man's idea of the perfect black leader, then the question "Would you like to be the new Booker T. Washington?" becomes highly ironic. It might suggest, "Would you like to be *our* man in Harlem?" Clearly, Ellison, if not the narrator, has a very ambivalent attitude toward Booker T. Washington.

The narrator accepts the job with the Brotherhood and is immediately given money to pay off his debts, buy new clothes, and change living places. He is to have a totally new identity with no connections whatsoever to the past. He is to leave Mary's, break contact with his parents, and learn his *new name*, which is handed to him in an envelope by Brother Jack—just as his other identities had been handed to him in envelopes by various people. He is to think of himself as being the new person.

The business over, the new brother is escorted back to the party and introduced to the others. A drunk white man at the piano asks the narrator to sing. After all, all black men sing black folk songs! The moment is extremely embarrassing. Brother Jack is furious and has the drunk brother removed from the room. The narrator, who might have taken offense, treats the matter lightly and the rest of the guests, obviously relieved, apologize for the attitude of their "backward" brother.

Throughout the party scene Ellison reminds you how limited and hypocritical most whites are in understanding and treatment of blacks. The drunk man, like many whites, assumes that the narrator can sing and entertain just because he's black. On the other hand, the more "advanced" whites assume that the narrator understands history, sociology, economics, and politics, without stopping to realize that white America has "done everything they can think of to prevent you from knowing" these things. The chapter closes with the narrator only partially aware of the darker side of the Brotherhood. He needs the money and the job, and he wants to speak. So he is willing to put up with their strange behavior, at least for a time. Later in the novel he will begin to see their real intent.

CHAPTER 15

The narrator spends his last night at Mary's and wakes up early the next morning to the sound of someone above him banging on the steam pipes. It is cold and there is no heat. The chorus of banging picks up, as others awaken, annoyed by the banging. The narrator's head is splitting from the drinking the night before, and he starts furiously on the pipes himself. Out of control, he grabs a cast-iron bank, shaped in the form of a "very black red-lipped and wide-mouthed Negro" and starts banging away. The head breaks, and the bank scatters its coins across the room. Mary hears him from outside and asks what is going on. He quickly sweeps the coins and broken metal into a pile, wraps them in a newspaper, and stuffs it in his overcoat pocket for later disposal.

NOTE: The symbolism of the bank   You will want to pay close attention to the bank, if you are interested in following Ellison's symbols, because the broken bank stays with the narrator from now until the end of the novel. The bank, like the Sambo dolls that Tod Clifton ends up selling, seems to represent a part of the black past that the narrator would like to hide. Its wide-grinning mouth eats coins. A coin is placed in the hand, and when a lever is thrown, the hand flips the coin into the grinning mouth. Does this suggest what "grinning Negroes" were willing to do for money from white masters? Remember the battle royal scene in Chapter 1 where the black boys scrambled for money on the electrified carpet? Is the narrator selling out to the Brotherhood for money? Keep this rich, complex symbol in mind as you follow it through.

The narrator has coffee with Mary, who seems unshakeably serene in the midst of all the noise. The narrator pulls out a hundred dollar bill and hands it to her in payment of his back rent, and she is overjoyed. She is proud she will be able to pay the bills everyone has been bothering her about. Did he win the money playing the numbers, she asks? Yes, he answers, relieved to find a simple explanation. He is not supposed to let her know he is leaving, nor that he is involved with the Brotherhood. She is so pleased about the money she seems totally unconcerned about what he's doing; so he is able to get his prized briefcase and leave. As he goes out he hears Mary singing the blues, as she always does. It seems to reassure her and bring her peace of mind.

A few blocks down the street he tries to throw the broken bank into a garbage can, but a woman stops him, yelling at him that she doesn't want any trash from "field niggers" in her garbage can. So he is forced to pluck it out. A few more blocks down the street, he just leaves it in the snow, hoping no one will notice, but someone picks it up and returns it to him, accusing him of being some kind of criminal making an illegal "drop." So he finally gives up and puts it in his briefcase, figuring that he will dispose of it later. Don't forget it's there, because it will reappear before the novel's end. The bank, as the previous note suggests, is a part of himself that he just can't get rid of.

The chapter ends with his arrival at his new home, a clean three-room apartment in a neutral, racially mixed neighborhood on the upper East Side. It is a neat, orderly, well-maintained world, just like the organization he has joined. He spends the remainder of the day in the apartment studying the pamphlets the Brotherhood has given him and preparing to make his first speech at a rally in Harlem that evening.

CHAPTER 16

Chapter 16 is an important and exciting chapter, consisting largely of the narrator's first speech for the Brotherhood and the reaction of the Brothers to it. The chapter is shot through with images of sight and blindness. Look for them as you read, and ask yourself what they are suggesting.

The narrator is driven by Brother Jack and some others to an arena in Harlem that is usually used for boxing matches. He remembers his father telling him how a famous boxer had been beaten blind in a fight in that arena, and the narrator notices the boxer's picture on the wall. He is nervous in his new blue suit, wondering how he will do and whether the people will like him. He paces up and down in the locker room, goes outside, then comes back in again, anxious to get started. Then Brother Jack gives the signal and they all march in, as the crowd sings "John Brown's body lies a mold'ring in the grave." The narrator's eyes are blinded by the spotlights as they move toward the stage.

The speeches begin. Each speaker touches on a different aspect of the problem. Then comes the narrator's turn. He is the one the crowd has been waiting for, the hero of the eviction protest, the young man who spoke and disappeared and then was found again by the Brotherhood.

At first he doesn't know what to do, but, as in the eviction speech, he follows instinct. He goes back to what he knows, the tradition of southern political oratory that he grew up with. "They think we're blind," he tells his audience. "Think about it, they've dispossessed us each of one eye from the day we're born. . . . We're a nation of one-eyed mice." Playing on the metaphor of blindness, he asks the members of his audience to join together and help one another to see better rather than using the one eye that each of them has to attack others. "Let's reclaim our sight; let's combine and spread our vision."

Moved by his own words and the response of the crowd, he becomes more personal. "I feel, I feel suddenly that I have become *more human*," he tells the crowd almost in a whisper. There is at that moment a special bond between the speaker and his audience, a bond that is personal and deeply emotional. He finishes, and the crowd goes wild. The brothers file from the stage, and Brother Jack is excited. But the reaction of the other brothers is not so positive. The narrator is stunned. The speech has been the greatest moment of his life, and the brothers are telling him that it was "a most unsatisfactory beginning."

Two of the brothers in particular—one identified as the man with the pipe and the other named Brother Wrestrum (whom we will meet again)—say that the speech is backward and reactionary. They tell the narrator and the other brothers that such emotional tactics are not in keeping with the scientific discipline of the Brotherhood. The people must be taught rationally to understand their role as part of the process of history. Emotional rabble-rousers like the narrator are simply of no use to the Brotherhood's design.

Brother Jack, who has listened carefully to both praise and criticism, finds a middle road. The new brother is to be trained. He will not be allowed to speak again until he is properly indoctrinated into the Brotherhood's philosophy and methods. He will be sent to Brother Hambro. The group agrees that the narrator is to begin training with Brother Hambro the next morning, and so he goes home, exhausted, disappointed that the brothers did not approve, but happy about his relationship with the people. As he lies in bed, trying to figure out what has happened, he wonders what he meant by the phrase "more human." Was it something he learned in college? He remembers an English teacher named Woolridge who taught him Joyce and Yeats and O'Casey, those great writers of the Irish Renaissance, and he remembers something Woolridge said: "Stephen's problem, like ours, was not actually one of creating the uncreated conscience of his race, but of creating the *uncreated features of his face*. . . .We create the race by creating ourselves. . . ."

NOTE: "The uncreated features of his face" Almost every critic who writes about *Invisible Man* discusses this phrase, which has become one of the most widely quoted lines from the novel. Stephen Dedalus, the hero of James Joyce's *A Portrait of the Artist as a Young Man*, leaves Ireland at the end of the novel to begin his task as an artist of creating "the uncreated conscience of my race." Ellison plays on Joyce's phrase by changing "conscience" to "features" and "race" to "face." Ellison is an individualist who believes that the job of each individual is to create himself, to become genuinely and honestly a single individual. Stephen wants to become a spokesman for the Irish people, his *race*, but Ellison does not want to be thought of just as a black writer. His hero is an individual in the act of creating himself, in the act of becoming a person, a "more human" person.

CHAPTER 17

There is a passage of four months. The narrator has been studying with Hambro, "a tall, friendly man, a lawyer and the Brotherhood's chief theoretician." Hambro is a hard teacher, but he is fair, and the narrator feels, as the chapter opens, that he is ready for whatever the Brotherhood wants him to do. He has attended meetings regularly all over the city, he has come to know the Brotherhood ideology well, and he has learned the discipline that is involved in working for the Brotherhood.

On the day the action of the chapter begins, Brother Jack calls the narrator and drives him to Harlem, where they talk in a bar. He informs the narrator that he has been appointed chief spokes-man of the Harlem district. The narrator is over-joyed. His dreams have been fulfilled. In this way he can work directly with his people. Brother Jack takes him to the office, introduces him to Brother Tarp, with whom he will be working, and reminds him to be there the next morning for a full com-mittee meeting.

The meeting begins promptly at nine, and all the committee members are there except for Brother Tod Clifton. As Brother Jack begins the meeting by announcing the narrator's appointment as chief spokesman, Clifton comes in, a bandage on his face covering a wound he received fighting one of Ras the Exhorter's men. He is late because he had to go to the doctor.

Who is Ras the Exhorter? He is a short, stout black man who has been organizing Harlem on a racist basis, preaching the gospel of black nation-alism, and sending his men to fight any organi-zation, like the Brotherhood, that advocates co-operation between blacks and whites. The conflict between the Brotherhood (represented by the nar-rator and Tod Clifton) and Ras the Exhorter serves as one of the central themes of the last third of the novel.

Tod Clifton and the narrator quickly become friends. Tod is an extremely handsome young black man who seems to carry in his genetic makeup the best features of both his African and Anglo-Saxon ancestry. He is a hard worker who welcomes the narrator as an ally. The narrator will organize the community leaders behind the Brotherhood's pol-icy of fighting against evictions, and Tod will or-ganize his youth groups to protect the narrator and other neighborhood speakers from being attacked on the street. Tod is excited about the plan for organizing Harlem. "It'll be bigger than anything since Garvey," he says.

NOTE: Marcus Garvey   Marcus Garvey (1887–1940) was a native of Jamaica who came to New York in 1916 and started a black nationalist movement, urging American blacks to return to Africa. Garvey had an estimated two million followers during the 1920s. He was convicted of mail fraud in 1925 and returned to Jamaica in 1927 after serving time in prison. Some of Ras the Exhorter's ideas are very similar to those of Garvey, though the Exhorter is in no way an attempt by Ellison to depict Marcus Garvey.

Tod and the narrator take to the streets and are forced almost immediately into a confrontation with Ras the Exhorter's men, who interrupt the narrator's first speech that evening. The narrator tackles one of Ras's men, and Tod goes after Ras himself. The narrator beats his man, then goes to help Tod, whom he finds in an alley lying on his back with Ras, knife in hand, standing over him. Helpless, the narrator is forced to watch and to listen.

Ras is a fascinating figure, and in this scene you may find him both appealing and repulsive at the same time. He is crazy and violent, but to many readers what he says makes sense. You will have to weigh the arguments on both sides carefully as you think about Ras. He *spares* Tod's life because he loves him, he admires him, and he wants him to come over to his side. He wants the narrator, too. He says that Tod is first of all an *African* and that in Africa a man as handsome and intelligent as Tod would be king. He stands over Tod with his knife, essentially arguing with him, trying to persuade him to come over to the Black Nationalist cause. These white men will betray you, Ras tells Tod. They will get rid of you when it suits their purpose, so don't trust them. He accuses Tod and the narrator of joining the Brotherhood so they can enjoy white women. He pleads with them to be part of black unity, to break entirely with any organization run by white men. What do you think of these arguments? They are very similar to those used by black militants in the 1960s, most notably the Black Muslims and the Black Panthers. The Communists did, in effect, betray the black members of the party who worked so hard during the 1930s, and this might suggest that Ras is right. What is Ellison supporting? Is it possible to know at this point in the novel? Keep these questions in mind as you continue reading.

Chapter 17 ends with a brief scene the next morning in the narrator's office. Brother Tarp comes in and hangs a picture of Frederick Douglass on the wall facing the narrator's desk. Douglass is Tarp's hero, and he wants the narrator to see him as he works.

NOTE: Frederick Douglass   Born a slave named Frederick Augustus Washington Bailey in 1817, this famous fighter for black rights ran away from his owner in 1838, ending up in Massachusetts, where he changed his name to Frederick Douglass. A brilliant speaker and writer, he devoted his life to work for the abolition of slavery and the elimination of racial discrimination. His autobiography, *Narrative* *of the Life of Frederick Douglass* (1845; revised 1881), is one of the great pieces of black American literature and became an inspiration to generations of blacks fighting for equality in America. Ellison's use of a variety of famous black leaders as possible models for the narrator is important. Booker T. Washington, Marcus Garvey, and Douglass represent three different paths for blacks to follow. Brother Tarp would like the narrator to imitate Frederick Douglass, and the narrator at the end of Chapter 17 finds the idea very exciting.

CHAPTER 18

Time passes, how much you don't know, but it seems to be at least a couple of months. The Brotherhood's work in Harlem is extraordinarily successful. The narrator's speeches and parades, the organization of the community's ministers and politicians, the enthusiasm of the people for the issue of evictions all combine to increase membership in the Brotherhood at a dizzying rate and make the narrator famous.

At the beginning of Chapter 18 the narrator receives an anonymous note telling him to slow down. The note says that the Brotherhood doesn't want him to be so famous. He will be cut down if he isn't careful. He is both angry and frightened. Who could have written it? It came in an envelope with no postage stamp. Does that mean it was an inside job? Who do you think sent the letter? Look for clues as you read the remainder of the chapter.

The narrator asks Brother Tarp how the members feel about him, and Tarp reminds him that his stress on interracial cooperation has led to the creation of a poster entitled "After the Struggle: The Rainbow of America's Future." Youth members have mounted the posters in subways, and people have begun hanging them in their homes. Tarp is impressed with the success of the narrator's work and reassures him that the people are behind him.

NOTE: Tarp's link of chain   As a symbol of his support for the narrator, Brother Tarp pulls from his pocket a worn metal link from a chain, and he gives it to the narrator as a token. Brother Tarp filed that chain from his own leg after nineteen years on the chain gang when, like Frederick Douglass, he headed north to start a new life. Because of those nineteen years given him as punishment for standing up and saying "no" to a white man, he still drags his foot even though there's nothing physically wrong with it. Old now and ready to retire, he wants to pass on that spirit of justice and integrity to the narrator. So he gives him that link of chain as a good-luck piece and as a reminder. The word "link" has at least two senses—literally, one of a group of loops making up a chain; figuratively, something that ties together past and present. The chain *links* the narrator to his own past, which he has forgotten, a past symbolized by Tarp's experience and by his grandfather, whom Tarp reminds him of. Taking the link makes the narrator remember his own childhood and hear the songs his parents and grandparents used to sing. He is reassured that he is doing the right thing. He likes the symbolism of the chain.

Later in the morning Brother Wrestrum comes into the office. He is disturbed by the link of chain sitting on the narrator's desk. He sees the link as an advertisement of the racial nature of the narrator's cause, a symbol that the white brothers might find offensive. He doesn't want to stress the cause of Harlem, of black people, but the cause of the Brotherhood. He wants all brothers to wear emblems that will identify them so that members of the Brotherhood won't end up fighting with each other. Wrestrum seems uneasy. Is he jealous of the narrator's success? Is he the one who wrote the letter?

While Wrestrum is in the office, the phone rings. It is the editor of a magazine, who wants to do an article on the narrator. The narrator says that Tod Clifton would be a much better person to interview, but Wrestrum insists that the narrator sit for the interview. Reluctantly, the narrator agrees. Two weeks later he will wish that he hadn't.

Two weeks after the meeting with Wrestrum, the narrator finds himself downtown at Brotherhood headquarters. With absolutely no warning, he is accused by Brother Wrestrum of being an individualist who is exploiting the Brotherhood for his own personal gain. Wrestrum accuses the narrator of trying to become a dictator in Harlem and of having had the article in the magazine published to glorify himself rather than the Brotherhood. The narrator replies that he hasn't even seen the article, and besides doesn't Brother Wrestrum know that he tried to have the interview done with Tod Clifton? Wrestrum himself was the one who urged the narrator to do it. What is going on? The narrator and Wrestrum argue and call each other names. The narrator is asked to leave the room, the charges are discussed, and he is brought back.

The decision of the committee is that, while the narrator has been found innocent on the charge of the magazine article, it will be best for the "good of the organization" that the narrator be removed from Harlem. He is given the choice of remaining inactive until further notice or of lecturing downtown on the Woman Question. This is all done seriously. Nobody laughs. The narrator is appalled. It's like a crazy dream, a nightmare, a strange joke. They can't be serious, but they are. Are you as surprised as the narrator? Why, when he is obviously doing so well, is he sent downtown to lecture on the Woman Question, something he knows *nothing* about? The narrator accepts the assignment because it is the only way he can continue to be active, but the chapter ends with him sneaking out of Harlem, afraid to tell his friends what has happened. His identity has been changed again, and again by someone else's choice.

CHAPTER 19

Chapter 19 is a transitional chapter, like Chapters 7 and 12. *Invisible Man* seems to be constructed in four major movements, each centering around a crisis. The crisis that begins the final movement comes in Chapter 20, when the narrator returns to Harlem to try to find Tod Clifton, who has disappeared. But before he returns to Harlem, he spends an evening with a white woman. That is the main action of Chapter 19.

As you read this chapter, ask yourself what Ellison is up to. Some readers think the chapter reads like something out of a torrid romance. Handsome black man speaks to a bunch of unsatisfied women about the "Woman Question," and what the women are really interested in is *biology*, not *ideology*. As the narrator tells the story of his seduction by the unnamed woman in red, whose husband appears to come home while she is in bed with him, you must wonder how seriously you are supposed to take all this. The narrator is *very* naive. When the woman goes off to change into something more comfortable and reappears in a red hostess gown, the narrator does not seem to get the message. He has come to her apartment for "coffee" and discussion after his lecture on the Woman Question, and she asks him, "Perhaps you'd prefer wine or milk instead of coffee?" The idea of milk turns him off, but he misses the oddness of the question.

Her change of clothes, her apartment with its life-size painting of a pink Renoir nude, her talk, her movement, her excitement over the "primitive" quality of the narrator, all mark the woman as one of Ellison's objects of satire. When one critic asked him if his depiction of the narrator's relationship with white women wasn't a weakness in the novel, Ellison chided the critic for taking both this scene and Chapter 24 too seriously. Perhaps you ought to be guided by Ellison's own judgment here and accept this sequence as a piece of tongue-in-cheek satire, based on the traditional myth that white women desire black men. Do you enjoy the humor of this chapter, or do you think that neither the narrator nor the scarlet woman is a very believable character in this scene?

Whether the scene is parody, satire, or serious writing, the appearance of the husband scares the narrator to death. He puts on his clothes, leaves,

and vows to keep "the biological and ideological"
apart in the future. He fears that the woman will
tell the Brotherhood about what he's done, but no
one ever says anything. So he goes on speaking
on the Woman Question until one evening the
phone rings and he's called to an emergency meeting. Tod Clifton has disappeared, and the narrator
is needed to return to Harlem immediately.

CHAPTER 20

When asked about the style of *Invisible Man* (see
the section Style for details), Ellison commented
that the style moved from realism to expressionism
to surrealism. As you read the last six chapters,
beginning with Chapter 20, think about what surrealism is and why the style might be described as
surrealistic. Something changes in the narrator
during Chapter 20, and he begins to move inward,
seeing the world outside from a new perspective.
What happens in Chapter 20 shakes him profoundly and makes him feel that the world outside
is unreal and that he is just awakening from a deep
sleep to see the world as it truly is for the first
time.

The whole chapter has an air of nightmare about
it. The narrator returns to Harlem in search of Tod
Clifton, but everything has changed. He goes to a
bar called Barrelhouse's Jolly Dollar, where he used
to meet one of his favorite contacts, Brother Maceo. When he gets there, not only is Maceo gone
but the men there resent being called "brother."
It's as if the whole movement has vanished since
he was sent downtown. He goes to his old office
in search of Brother Tarp, but Tarp has disappeared, and the portrait of Frederick Douglass has

been taken down. "Returning to the district was like returning to a city of the dead."

The next morning he finds a number of the members and asks them about Tod Clifton, but no one knows anything about Tod's disappearance. He goes back downtown to attend a committee meeting and discovers that it not only has started without him but that he hasn't been invited. The entire Harlem program has fallen apart and he has been sent to do a job with no help, no instructions, and no official program. Why? Unable to figure out what to do, he wanders over to Fifth Avenue and buys a new pair of summer shoes. Then he walks down Forty-third Street toward Sixth Avenue where he encounters a strange and remarkable sight.

A crowd is gathered in front of a piece of cardboard on which "a grinning doll of orange-and-black tissue paper with thin flat cardboard disks forming its head and feet" is dancing. Something behind the cardboard is making the doll dance, and that "something" is saying:

> *Shake it up! Shake it up!*
> *He's Sambo, the dancing doll, ladies and gentlemen. . . .*
> *He'll keep you entertained. He'll make you weep sweet—*
> *Tears from laughing.*
> *Shake him, shake him, you cannot break him. . . .*

NOTE: Sambo the dancing doll Both the name and the movements of the doll are important. Like the grinning bank that the narrator finds in his room at Mary Rambo's, the Sambo doll is one of the central symbols of the novel. "Sambo," like "Uncle Tom," is a term used by blacks to describe other blacks who allow themselves to be used and manipulated by whites. If an "Uncle Tom" is a black man who lets himself be used as a servant by whites, a "Sambo" is a black man who plays the role of comedian or mindless entertainer. He is a black who grins and laughs and pretends that he doesn't mind what is being done to him. He is the professional funny man, the song-and-dance man, who entertains whites and seems not to mind the hurt and pain that blacks must suffer, in part because of his own failure to do anything. Thus the grinning Sambo bank at Mary's and the dancing Sambo doll symbolize the very type of black man that both the Brotherhood and Ras the Exhorter seem to be fighting against.

The sight of the dancing doll and the comic spiel of the manipulator of the doll attract the narrator's attention, but what stuns him is his discovery of who the street merchant is. It is Tod Clifton. The narrator cannot believe his eyes. Why? Why would Tod give up the Brotherhood and "plunge outside history" (to use Tod's own phrase) to become a cheap entertainer, a seller of Sambo dolls?

The narrator comes to no answer. Remember that this is a first-person narration and that the narrator was not present in Harlem when Tod made his decision. Like the narrator, you can never know—you can only guess. One guess is that Tod felt betrayed by the Brotherhood when he discovered that it had changed its emphasis from local programs such as that in Harlem to more international issues. This is precisely what the Communist party did around 1940 and 1941, thus disillusioning American blacks who were working with it. Perhaps Tod simply despaired of achieving anything and gave up. Or perhaps he gave up because he thought the narrator had betrayed the cause and he was disillusioned by the narrator's disappearance. Which is the most likely explanation as far as you are concerned?

Whatever the reason, the narrator can't look at him or bring himself to talk to him. Then Tod's lookout warns him to move: The police are coming, and Tod has no license to sell these dolls. Tod and the crowd vanish around the corner, leaving the narrator to think about what has happened. The narrator picks up a doll that has been left on the sidewalk and puts it in his pocket with Brother Tarp's chain link (an interesting combination). Then he goes off after Tod. He sees him again on Forty-second Street, being led away by a cop. The cop pushes him along, and suddenly Tod whirls and uppercuts the policeman. The policeman goes down, draws his gun, and shoots Ted. The narrator, across the street, is frozen in horror.

The narrator tries to reach Tod but is stopped by another policeman, who insults him, calling him "Junior." "I'm his friend," the narrator says, but it is no use. They will not let him through. In a few moments Tod is dead. He has become what the name "Tod" means in German. The narrator answers the policeman's questions about Tod and then wanders toward the subway after the body is taken away in a police wagon.

He is in a state of shock. Nothing makes sense. Why should Tod deliberately court his own death like that? Tod knew better. He was street-wise and knew what white policemen did to any black who resisted. Did he want to die? Again, these questions are not answered. They are only food for your thought and the thought of the narrator, who tries to puzzle out what has happened as he waits for a train to take him back to Harlem.

A change comes over him. He starts to notice details that had escaped him before. He sees three boys dressed up in summer suits and felt hats, and he realizes that he has never *seen* boys like this before. He has never thought of these boys or of women like Mary Rambo or younger women who walked the streets in "dark exotic-colored stockings." He has been so busy with historical issues he has not really noticed people as individuals. Who speaks for such people, and who will speak for Tod? These are the questions he asks himself as the chapter ends. He realizes that he is finally waking up to reality. "I'd been asleep, dreaming," he thinks. But he is making a start. The death of Tod Clifton has stirred him to see people as people for the first time. The last major movement of the novel has begun.

CHAPTER 21

The narrator returns to Harlem and continues to reflect on Tod Clifton's death. He goes over his own actions and wonders if he isn't in some way responsible. He asks himself how to restore the integrity of Tod Clifton, and he comes to the conclusion that it must be done through his funeral. They will have a massive funeral for Tod, and his death will become a means of reuniting the community. He gathers together the district members and organizes his campaign of protest against the brutality that destroyed Tod Clifton. Signs reading BROTHER TOD CLIFTON/OUR HOPE SHOT DOWN are posted throughout the community.

The funeral is held outdoors in Mount Morris Park to attract the largest possible crowd, and people come from all over the city. Rich and poor, brothers and sisters, and nonmembers of the Brotherhood alike want to mourn for a man everybody loved. Bands play muted funeral marches, and an old man begins singing the familiar hymn, "There's Many a Thousand Gone." Another man joins in on the euphonium, a brass instrument like the tuba, and then the crowd, black and white alike, begins to sing. It is a special moment in the novel, one you will savor. The narrator himself is deeply moved: "Something deep had shaken the crowd, and the old man and the man with the horn had done it. They had touched upon something deeper than protest, or religion. . . ." Music, the music of the Negro spiritual tradition going back to slavery, speaks to the heart in a way that the scientific theory of the Brotherhood never can. It touches and humanizes the narrator and gives him a sense of unity with all people, not just with those who are part of the movement.

In this mood, the narrator gives Tod Clifton's funeral oration, much as Mark Antony in Shakespeare's *Julius Caesar* speaks for Caesar in that play. Just as Antony says he comes to bury Caesar, not to praise him, the narrator keeps saying that Tod Clifton is dead and that there is nothing he can say that will make any difference. His speech is simple and honest and moving: It comes to no political conclusions. He speaks not as a brother to a mass of people but as an individual to individuals. He mourns for the unnecessary death of a man he loved, and he tells the people that Tod Clifton stands for all of them. "He's in the box and we're in there with him, and when I've told you this you can go.

It's dark in this box and it's crowded. It has a cracked ceiling and a clogged toilet in the hall.'' The people know. The narrator does not have to tell them: Tod Clifton is any black person who was shot down because he could not stand it in the box any longer.

The funeral ends. The crowd, moved to deep feeling but not to any specific action, goes home, and the narrator feels again the tension and knows that "something had to be done before it simmered away in the heat."

CHAPTER 22

This is an extremely important chapter. The action that began in Chapter 20 with the death of Tod Clifton comes to a climax as the narrator confronts the committee after the funeral. For the first time since he joined the Brotherhood, he has acted on his own volition. He has done something not because someone told him to, but because he chose to. He knows from the moment he arrives at the meeting that he is going to be attacked, but he maintains his integrity before them. He acted, he tells the committee, on "my personal responsibility." "Your what?" Brother Jack asks. "My personal responsibility," he says again. Immediately we are reminded of Chapter 1 and the battle royal scene where he was making his speech and was reprimanded for suggesting that blacks try to gain social equality. Again he is being attacked by white men for presuming to act on his own initiative, especially by Brother Tobitt, who is exactly what his name suggests, a "twobit" character, who thinks he's superior to other white men because he has a black wife.

The narrator stands up under the attacks of

Brother Tobitt and Brother Jack. He believes he has done right, even though Jack calls Tod Clifton a Brutus (that is, a betrayer of Caesar, or the Brotherhood). To the narrator, Tod's defection from the Brotherhood is not important. What is important is that he was shot because he was black. Brother Jack is not interested in the problems of the black man any more. Clifton was a traitor to the Brotherhood. Therefore, Brother Jack reasons, he is not to be praised by Brotherhood members. The narrator has reasoned it out differently, because he has thought for himself. "You were not hired to think," Brother Jack says firmly. And the narrator knows where he stands. This *is* the truth about the Brotherhood. They don't want his mind, only his mindless obedience to *their* policies.

The tension grows as the argument between the narrator and Brother Jack becomes more and more fierce. Brother Jack tells the narrator that demonstrations are no longer effective and that they should be discontinued. The narrator wants to know who gives Brother Jack the right to speak for black people. "Who are you, anyway," he asks, "the great white father?" Then he drives the point home: "Wouldn't it be better if they called you Marse Jack?"

At this, the usually cool, rational Jack loses his poise. He leaps to his feet as if to attack the narrator, and suddenly an object like a marble drops to the table. Jack grabs it and throws it into his water glass. Brother Jack has only one good eye. The left one is a glass eye.

NOTE: Brother Jack's glass eye It is worth pausing over this fascinating piece of symbolism.

Throughout the novel Ellison has been working with images of sight and blindness. The narrator up to now hasn't really seen what has been going on around him. In his first speech for the Brotherhood he spoke of black people as "one-eyed mice," the other eye having been put out by white men. Jack is one-eyed also, the other eye having been closed by the Brotherhood. He cannot see anything except what the Brotherhood permits him to see. He has literally sacrificed his eye for the Brotherhood. In this chapter, when the narrator finally sees how limited Jack's vision is, he expands his own vision. He, as it were, opens his eyes for the first time, realizing that Jack has never seen him, never really acknowledged his existence as a human being.

The death of Tod Clifton, the funeral, and the argument with the committee have changed the narrator. As the chapter ends, he concludes, "After tonight I wouldn't ever look the same, or feel the same." His identity is changed once more, evolving into something more like a true self.

CHAPTER 23

The narrator is sent to Brother Hambro for instructions about the new policies of the Brotherhood. On his way downtown he runs into Ras the Exhorter, the last person he wants to see. Ras attacks him for doing nothing about the shooting and demands to know what the Brotherhood has to say for itself. The narrator has no answer, and he leaves, followed by two of Ras' men who attempt to beat him up in front of a movie theater.

The movie doorman intervenes, and the narrator escapes temporarily. His problem is how to keep Ras' men from harassing him, now that the Brotherhood organization has fallen apart.

All at once he notices three men in "natty cream-colored summer suits" and wearing dark glasses. An idea comes to him. He goes into a drugstore and buys himself some dark glasses. Immediately everything changes. The world looks green through the glasses, and a woman comes up to him and calls him "Rinehart." He answers, and she realizes from his voice that he isn't Rinehart, but the mistake has been made. He has learned from the woman that Rinehart usually wears a hat, so he goes to a hat shop and buys a wide-brimmed white hat to go with his glasses, and as if by magic a couple of men on the street call him Rinehart. He even walks by Ras the Exhorter, who has now changed his name to the DESTROYER, and is not recognized. He decides to test the disguise even further by going to the Jolly Dollar, and even Barrelhouse, the Bartender, and Brother Maceo mistake him for Rinehart. He ends up—as Rinehart—having a fight with Maceo and getting thrown out of the bar.

Who is this Rinehart, anyway? Out on the street a woman comes up to him and asks him for the day's last number. A police car stops and asks him for the usual police payoff. Rinehart seems to be some kind of a con man, a numbers runner, a gambler. A beautiful girl comes up to him and starts to seduce him until she realizes he isn't Rinehart. Apparently Rinehart is quite a lover, too. The narrator runs off and finds himself in front of a store that has been converted into a church. The minister's name is the Rev. B. P. Rinehart, and a member of the congregation comes up to the narrator on the street, mistaking him for this minister.

NOTE: What does all this mean?   You may wish to consult The Characters section under "Rinehart" for some analysis of this strange and elusive figure. Much can be said about him because everything Ellison does here with Rinehart is open to interpretation. Is he real? Is he one person? Is he several people? You don't know. You do know that he is, for Ellison, a symbol of life in the real world. He is a man who can live in the chaos of reality and survive by simply adapting to it and taking advantage of it. Rinehart represents another possibility for the narrator—a strategy for coping with reality that from here to the end of the novel he will call "Rinehartism." We might define it as a kind of cynical opportunism. It's another identity that a man *can* adopt, and Rinehart, with his magical hat and glasses, seems to be protected against the hurt of the world. He is in control.

Whatever Rinehart represents, the narrator is not quite ready to deal with it. "I caught a brief glimpse of the possibilities posed by Rinehart's multiple personalities and turned away. It was too vast and confusing to contemplate." The narrator wants some order and structure in his life. That is why he joined the Brotherhood in the first place. So he puts away the hat and glasses and goes to see Hambro. Hambro is honest and brutal. When the narrator asks him why his district is being allowed to fall apart, Hambro answers simply, "We are making temporary alliances with other political groups and the

interests of one group of brothers must be sacrificed to that of the whole." The philosophy of the
Brotherhood is purely utilitarian: Do what is best
for the whole. If some suffer, that is unfortunate
but necessary. Individuals are not important. They
are merely part of the whole. The narrator argues
with Hambro, calling this view of individuals just
another form of Rinehartism. Of course Hambro
doesn't know who Rinehart is. The narrator begins
to see the situation even more clearly than he had
in the previous chapter. "Hambro looked as though
I were not there." To Hambro, the narrator is an
invisible man. "Well, I *was*," he says, "and yet I
was invisible, that was the fundamental contradic-
tion. I was and yet I was unseen."

The narrator leaves Hambro's and goes home to
think through the day's experiences. He is exhausted. He has been through the funeral, the
grueling fight with the committee, the experience
with Ras the Exhorter, the strange disguise as
Rinehart, and the discussion with Brother Hambro. His mind is trying to sort it all out. He realizes
that he was always invisible—to Norton, to Emerson, to Bledsoe, to Jack, to everyone. Only now
he knows it. Before he had been nothing because
he was nothing to himself. Now, though he is invisible to others, he is a self.

With this insight he comes to a decision. At last
he understands the meaning of the event with
which Chapter 1 began, the deathbed advice of his
grandfather. His grandfather had said, "I want you
to overcome 'em with yeses, undermine 'em with
grins, agree 'em to death and destruction, let 'em
swoller you till they vomit or bust wide open."

His grandfather's words have haunted him all
his life, but until now they only made him feel

uncomfortable. He has never either understood or believed in what his grandfather had said. Now he does. And he decides to follow that advice. He will stay in the Brotherhood, but he will be a spy in their midst, yessing them to death and destruction while he pretends to be a loyal worker. He will pretend to be an Uncle Tom, but in reality he will seek to undermine them. He plans to begin the next day by using their women as a source of information about them. He has a new purpose.

CHAPTER 24

The chapter opens on the day following the crisis with the Brotherhood, and the narrator puts his plan of "yessing them to death" into effect right away. He openly lies to the brothers at Headquarters about what is going on in Harlem, simply telling them what they want to hear and being pleasant and outwardly cooperative while getting on with his plan of undermining the organization. He decides that he needs a woman as a source of information and thinks of Emma, Brother Jack's mistress, whom he met at the Chthonian on the first night. He decides against her because she might be loyal to Jack and picks instead a woman named Sybil, whom he invites to his apartment the next night.

NOTE: Sybil   The name "Sybil," like nearly all the names in the novel, has symbolic meaning. A sibyl was a woman in Greek times who served as an oracle or prophet for one of the gods. The sibyls would make prophetic utterances when under divine inspiration. Inspiration could be easily confused with drunkenness. Ellison's Sybil seems like a complete failure as a prophetess. The narrator gets her drunk and asks for information about the Brotherhood, and this Sybil knows nothing. She only wants the narrator's body.

The evening with Sibyl becomes a series of ludicrous jokes. Like the woman in red from Chapter 19, Sybil has the illusion that the narrator is some sort of superman. She expects him to be a combination of the boxing champion Joe Louis and the noted actor and singer Paul Robeson. She wants to be raped by him in order to fulfill her white woman's fantasy of being violated by a black man. Apparently Sybil has always heard that white women want black men. So she wants what she assumes every other white woman wants, but what she wants is a myth. It doesn't exist. And to emphasize the point, Ellison has the narrator grab her lipstick and write on her belly, "SYBIL, YOU WERE RAPED BY SANTA CLAUS. SURPRISE." The myth of the black stud is on the same level as that of Santa Claus. It's a child's fantasy to be outgrown.

Sybil never outgrows it. She falls into a drunken sleep and wakes up thinking that something wonderful has happened to her while she was sleeping. She continues to think the narrator is perfectly wonderful, calling him "boo'ful" in her drunken stupor. The phone rings, jarring the narrator back to reality. It is someone from the district. All hell has broken loose in Harlem, and the narrator is needed at Morningside Heights.

He struggles to get Sybil dressed, grabs his briefcase, puts Sybil in a taxi, and starts walking toward Harlem. When he gets to 110th Street, he finds

Sybil "waiting beneath a street lamp, waving." She runs away, then falls in the street, totally unable to control herself. He gets another taxi and orders the driver to take her straight home. Then he flags down a bus and rides it to 125th Street and Riverside Drive. He can't seem to do anything right, for he has even taken the wrong bus, and now he will have to walk across 125th Street to Harlem.

CHAPTER 25

When he reaches Morningside Heights, the riot is in full force. Four men are running toward him pushing a safe, and he is caught with them in police fire. He falls to the pavement, hit by a bullet, and feels blood on his face. It is only a superficial wound, though. A slug has creased his head.

He finds himself in a nightmare world, unable to take care of himself. Then, for no reason, a man named Scofield helps him, and the narrator finds himself following Scofield and Dupre, the leader of a group of local blacks. They are planning something. They go to a hardware store, get flashlights, and then buckets which they fill with coal oil. Dupre seems to have organized everything. They take the buckets to a tenement house and clear the house of women and children. Scofield tells the narrator, "This is the place where most of us live." Nothing in the narrator's experience has prepared him for this. He is amazed. These people need no Brotherhood. No leaders. They are taking their lives into their own hands. The narrator thinks, "They organized it and carried it through alone; the decision is their own and their own action."

The people spread the oil, light it, and the building goes up in flames. Suddenly in the street, someone recognizes the narrator and calls him by his Brotherhood name. He runs, afraid that Ras' men will find him, and ends up in another rain of pistol fire. Dupre and Scofield have guns and are fighting it out with the police. But, the narrator suddenly sees that this battle is pure suicide—a few pistols against the police arsenal. Is this what the Brotherhood wanted, to have blacks fighting one another and the police in a riot which will ultimately mean self-destruction?

The narrator runs again in the nightmare of the streets littered with broken glass. There are looters everywhere, taking what they can, and as the narrator runs he sees a white body hanging from a lamp post. Have they lynched a white woman? No, it is another macabre joke. It is a dummy, a store mannequin.

Again, the narrator runs, and this time straight into Ras the Destroyer. Ras, surrounded by his men and carrying a shield and spear, is riding toward him on a huge black horse. The narrator searches for his dark glasses, his Rinehart disguise, but they have broken in his briefcase. So he must face Ras. Ras flings his spear at him and misses, hitting one of the mannequins behind him. The narrator grabs the spear and speaks, trying to hold back the tide of destruction. "They want this to happen," he says, trying to explain that he now sees through the Brotherhood. And even as he speaks, he knows it is too late. Ras and his men want to hang the narrator as a symbol. They would like to lynch him as whites lynched blacks. But the narrator is not ready to die. "I knew that it was better to live out one's own absurdity," he says, "than to die for that of others, whether for Ras's or Jack's."

NOTE: "To live out one's own absurdity." *Invisible Man* was published in 1952, at the height of the influence of French existentialist writing in the United States. The concept of absurdity, central to existentialists like Jean-Paul Sartre and Albert Camus, certainly influenced Ellison strongly. In this passage, the narrator comes to what might be called an existential affirmation. He realizes that life is absurd, that the organizations to which he has given himself are meaningless, but that the individual can *live*, can affirm his own existence in the face of that absurdity. We can live and choose to be an authentic self whether the universe has meaning or not. You might wish to read some existentialist literature, such as Camus' *The Stranger*, Sartre's *No Exit* and *Nausea*, and explore its influence on this novel, especially on this chapter and the Prologue and Epilogue.

Spurred by the will to live, he throws the spear back at Ras and fights his way through the crowd, using his briefcase and Tarp's leg chain as weapons. He is through with everything. All he wants is to get away, to find his way back to Mary's and be taken care of. He wants to say, ". . . we're all black folks together," but it's too late and the violence has spread everywhere out of control. He runs until exhausted, then stops to rest behind a hedge, where he hears people talking about Ras and his final battle with the police: Ras charging the cops like some crazy knight of old, fighting with spear and shield.

He gets up to run again, to find Jack and Tobitt and Wrestrum, when he sees two young white men in civilian clothes. Cops, he thinks, until he sees one holding a baseball bat. They want his briefcase, and he takes off down the street running. Suddenly he falls through an open manhole into what seems to be a coal cellar. The whites can't see him because he's a black man lying in the dark on a black heap of coal. He is now *literally* invisible, and they clamp the manhole cover back on, leaving him there, where he stays in a kind of tomb, a kind of living death, to sleep until morning.

The novel has come full circle. This is the underground home that the narrator refers to in the Prologue. This is where he has remained and written his novel since the night of the riot, slowly converting his dark into light, not knowing for a long time whether it was night or day. That process of lighting his way out of both the literal and figurative darkness of the underground cave begins at the conclusion of this chapter with the narrator's first act after he wakes up. He has no light to see his way out, and so "I realized that to light my way out I would have to burn every paper in the brief case." Notice what he burns and in what order: first, the high school diploma, then Clifton's doll, then the anonymous letter written by Brother Jack, then the slip of paper on which Jack had written his Brotherhood name. These are his white identities, all of which must be burned away, destroyed, before he can "light his way" out of the darkness of the cave.

NOTE: The briefcase and its contents The briefcase is the only object the narrator takes into the cave from his former life. He burns all the papers, but still in the briefcase is Mary's broken bank and its coins along with Tarp's leg chain. These two objects are part of his black heritage, a part that will always be with him. Perhaps these cannot or should not be left behind. What do you think? What about the briefcase itself? What might it represent?

The chapter ends with an agonizing dream in which the narrator is castrated by Emerson, Jack, Bledsoe, Norton and Ras, who laugh at him as he realizes that this is the price of freedom. This is what it has cost him to see reality. Now he is free of illusion, but he cannot go back to the real world. He must stay in the cave. "Here, at least, I could try to think things out in peace, or, if not in peace, in quiet. I would take up residence underground. The end was in the beginning."

EPILOGUE

The Prologue and Epilogue are harder to deal with than the rest of the book, because in the sense of "story," nothing happens. In one sense, the story line is at an end. But in an important sense the novel isn't over, if you think of things happening inside people's minds as well as externally. The most important things that happen to individuals are sometimes the interior things, the changes that take place within. That is what happens in the Epilogue. The story in *Invisible Man* is summed up by the narrator when he says, in the Epilogue's first paragraph, "I'm an invisible man and it placed me in a hole—or showed me the hole I was in. . . ." That's an effective metaphor. The hole he falls in at the end of Chapter 25 is where his life led him. But people can change. The German philosopher Friedrich Nietzsche said, "The snake that does not shed its skin will perish." During the course of writing the novel (the story of *Invisible Man*), the narrator learns that he must shed his figurative skin. He must give up his old identities; then, after he has had time to get used to who he really is, he must stop hibernating. Just as the bear comes out of his cave in the spring, just as the snake returns to the world after he has grown his new skin, the narrator must give up his invisibility and rejoin the world: "The hibernation is over. I must shake off the old skin and come up for breath," he says—using three metaphors at once.

But, you might ask, what does coming up and rejoining the world mean? He tells you. He will become involved in the world with his new knowledge. Even if it hurts, he will be part of the world because "even an invisible man has a socially responsible role to play." Staying in the cave is like dying. If you stay too long, then you can never come up. So he will, he says, as the novel ends, come up and play a role in a world he now understands is *better* because it is diversified. "America is woven of many strands," he reminds you, and "our fate is to become one, and yet many." That is why Ras is wrong and Brother Jack is wrong and Bledsoe is wrong and Emerson and Norton are wrong, because they deny the individual his right to be one and be different and still be part of the many. That is Ellison's final thought, and that is one thing that the narrator learns through his journey underground. That is what he will attempt to teach others. "Perhaps," the novel ends, "on the lower frequencies I speak for you." And he has, indeed, spoken for many in the last thirty years.

A STEP BEYOND

Tests and Answers

TESTS

Test 1

1. The "battle royal" where the black boys are _____
   made to fight each other symbolizes
   A. the backwardness of southern blacks
      as compared with northern blacks
   B. the way whites manipulate blacks by
      turning them against one another
   C. the way things were in small southern
      towns 50 years ago

2. The narrator gets his identity in the first _____
   quarter of the novel by following the model
   of
   A. the Founder and Dr. Bledsoe
   B. his grandfather and Jim Trueblood
   C. Mr. Norton and Mr. Emerson

3. The letters of recommendation that Dr. _____
   Bledsoe gives to the narrator really say
   A. "Keep This Nigger-Boy Running"
   B. "Blacks and Whites Can Become One"
   C. "Separate But Equal Is Best"

4. The narrator's experience at Liberty Paints _____
   suggests that
   A. whites use blacks to enhance their
      own superiority
   B. American businesses were opposed to
      unionization

C. the narrator ought to work for a
   company owned by black people

5. The Brotherhood represents   ——
   A. white "do-gooders"
   B. the Communist party
   C. "the brotherhood of man"

6. The turning point at the center of the novel   ——
   is the narrator's
   A. witnessing of an eviction of two old
      people
   B. decision that he has made a mistake
      in coming North
   C. decision to move from Men's House
      to Mary Rambo's

7. Brother Jack's character is symbolized by   ——
   his
   A. limp   B. glass eye
   C. business suit

8. Ras the Exhorter's ultimate goal is to   ——
   A. make blacks and whites equal
   B. have all blacks return to the South
   C. keep blacks and whites totally
      separate

9. The death of Tod Clifton is   ——
   A. totally the fault of white society
   B. secretly brought about by the
      Brotherhood
   C. in part the result of Tod's own despair
      of finding answers

10. The narrator ends up in a deserted coal cel-   ——
    lar where he

    A. plans to work to alleviate racism
    B. tries to think through the things in his
       life that got him there
    C. plots revenge against Bledsoe,
       Norton, and the Brotherhood

11. Explore the theme of "invisibility" in *Invisible Man*.

12. Write an essay on the symbolic use of names in the novel.

13. What view of white people emerges from a reading of *Invisible Man*?

14. Would you view *Invisible Man* as a "black" novel or a "universal" novel? Give evidence from the novel to support your opinion.

15. Analyze the role of black folk materials (jazz, Negro spirituals, folktales, dialect humor, etc.) in *Invisible Man*.

Test 2

1. The narrator is expelled from the college   _____
   because he
    A. behaved improperly with a white man
    B. exposed aspects of black life Dr.
       Bledsoe wanted to keep hidden
    C. was guilty of insubordination with Dr.
       Bledsoe

2. Young Mr. Emerson reveals the contents   _____
   of the letter to the narrator
    A. because he feels guilty about what the
       white world is doing to blacks
    B. because he personally despised
       Bledsoe

   C. in order to get revenge on his father,
      whom he resents

3. The narrator's encounters on the street with   _____
Peter Wheatstraw and later the yam seller
   A. suggest the importance of forgetting
      the past
   B. remind him that his southern folk
      heritage is part of his identity
   C. reinforce the hopelessness of the black
      situation in New York

4. Ellison's style in the novel   _____
   A. moves from realism to expressionism
      to surrealism
   B. moves from surrealism to realism
   C. is predominantly realistic throughout
      the novel

5. The character of the protagonist is such that   _____
he might be described as a
   A. reliable narrator
   B. naive narrator
   C. prejudiced narrator

6. The member of the Brotherhood most   _____
faithful to the narrator and his work in Harlem is
   A. Brother Wrestrum   B. Brother Tarp
   C. Brother Tobitt

7. The Brotherhood is opposed to the narra-   _____
tor's emotional and personal style of speaking because
   A. they are afraid the crowds will get out
      of control

B. it does not reflect their scientific, rational philosophy

C. it makes the other speakers look bad

8. The dancing Sambo dolls being sold by Tod   _____
Clifton
   A. are symbols of American commercialism
   B. suggest the way many blacks have behaved for whites in America
   C. suggest the good humor and comic nature of American blacks

9. The identity of Rinehart   _____
   A. gives the narrator the opportunity to make major reforms
   B. allows the narrator to undermine Ras the Exhorter
   C. allows the narrator to survive in a world of chaos and confusion

10. The decision of the narrator to leave his   _____
cave at the end of the novel symbolizes
   A. his failure to learn anything from his experiences
   B. the end of contemplation and the beginning of action
   C. his compromises in order to survive in life

11. Explore the symbolic use of the colors "black" and "white" in the novel.

12. What view of American blacks emerges from the reading of *Invisible Man*?

13. Would you view *Invisible Man* as an optimistic or pessimistic statement about the human situation? Why?

14. Analyze the development of the narrator as a character. How does he change during the course of the novel?

15. Discuss the imagery of sight and blindness in *Invisible Man*.

ANSWERS

Test 1
1. B   **2.** A   **3.** A   **4.** A   **5.** B   **6.** A
7. B   **8.** C   **9.** C   **10.** B

11. You might begin by carefully rereading the Prologue and Epilogue. Here the narrator defines "invisibility" clearly and discusses some of the consequences of being invisible. Many of the later chapters, especially Chapters 22, 23, and 25, develop the theme of invisibility in different ways. It is important to note that the narrator becomes more aware of his invisibility as he becomes more experienced; thus the closing chapters are more important in a study of this theme because it is here that the narrator develops a true perception of his condition. You may wish to explore the relationship between invisibility and the narrator's decision to stay in his cave. Will he still be an invisible man when he comes up and returns to the real world?

Two main directions you might take stem from the two major strands of the theme: (1) the idea that invisibility derives from white people not being able to *see* black people, and (2) the idea that invisibility is one's own fault, that it stems from a person's refusal to develop his own identity. The sections on "Themes" and the "Prologue" in this study guide may be of particular help to you as you sort out these two aspects of the invisibility theme. Which do you think is Ellison's major emphasis? There is evidence in the novel to support both. White behavior reinforces (1) and the behavior of the narrator reinforces (2).

12. This topic could produce a rather lengthy paper if you try to do *all* the names. So you might wish to select some of the more important ones and use them to illustrate Ellison's method. See The Characters section for the names of major characters. Names of most minor characters and place names are treated in the notes for the chapter where the name makes its first appearance.

Generally Ellison uses names that are symbolic rather than realistic. The symbolism may be drawn from a variety of sources. Sometimes the symbolism comes from a play on words like "Bledsoe" and "bleeds so" or "Wrestrum" and "rest room" or "Tobitt" and "two bit." A second source for symbolism in names is mythology and literature. Ellison chooses names that have historical, mythological, literary, or archetypal significance. Some examples are Chthonian (the hotel where the Brotherhood meets), Ras (also a play on words), Emerson, the Founder, and Jim Trueblood.

13. Ellison's treatment of whites makes a particularly interesting essay topic because it allows you to explore the kind of social statement this novel makes about the burden of blame white people bear for the condition of blacks in America. The white characters that you see may be broken mainly into two groups: (1) the trustees and businessmen and (2) the members of the Brotherhood. The first group includes Norton and Emerson, the second group Jack, Tobitt, and Hambro. There is also the terrible Mr. Kimbro at Liberty Paints.

As with his black characters, Ellison does not treat his whites merely as types. He does not reduce them to caricatures. If they are in many ways to blame for black conditions, they are still human beings. Their major fault as a group is to view black people as conveniences to be used. Remember the distinction made in this study guide between I-You relations and I-It relations. All whites have the tendency to use black people as Its. The trustees and the Brotherhood members are members of groups, of classes. They think they are "helping" blacks, when in reality they are helping their own groups or classes through their activities with blacks.

The section in this guide on The Characters and the appropriate Notes from the story section for those white characters not treated under The Characters should be useful. The whole section of the novel that takes place at Liberty Paints (Chapters 10 and 11) is a kind of symbolic portrait of white America. You may find a rereading of those chapters most helpful.

14. *Invisible Man* has been a very popular novel among both blacks and whites for more than three decades. It has survived the existentialism of the 1950s, the black protest movement of the 1960s, and the feminism of the 1970s. Something about it seems to appeal to young people, no matter what their race, their historical situation, or their geographic region. "Who knows but that, on the lower frequencies, I speak for you?" asks the narrator as the very last sentence of the novel. Does the narrator speak for *you*, whether you are black or white, old or young, male or female? That might be the topic of your essay.

If you want to defend *Invisible Man* as a universal novel, it might be wise to concentrate on the narrator. Is he a character you identify with? What sorts of problems does he have that are also your problems? What sorts of dreams and hopes does he have that are also your dreams and hopes? You might follow him through the course of the novel and review his quest for identity, his search for a self that is meaningful. Is that search a universal search?

Is his growing up, his testing through a series of trials, mistakes, and missteps, something that all young men and women go through? What, in your personal experience, might parallel the narrator's adventures?

If you want to stress *Invisible Man* as a black novel, then you will want to look most closely at those aspects of the narrator's experience that seem *least* universal and most limited to what a black man would go through. Are there aspects of his experience that, as a white or oriental, for example, you *cannot* identify with?

15. This topic has been widely studied. Robert O'Meally and Raymond Olderman (see Critical Works under Further Reading) are very helpful. Under the heading of black folk materials you might include music, especially jazz, the blues, spirituals, and gospel music. You might also include folktales such as those of Brer Rabbit and Brer Bear and the use of traditional black storytelling such as that of Jim Trueblood in Chapter 2. Black dialect characters like Peter Wheatstraw and the yam seller supply still other examples of Ellison's use of black folk materials.

When some or all of these elements are studied together, certain patterns appear. When the narrator attends college, he tries to become educated in such a way that he can be accepted in the white man's world. He goes to New York and doesn't want to be thought of as an uneducated, inexperienced black boy from the South who doesn't know his way around. So he avoids the language, food, music, and clothes associated with that southern past. He tries to *be* white. In the Brotherhood, he also avoids black styles and customs. Later in the novel, as he begins to develop a self, an identity of his own, he begins to see that these aspects of his past are important. In his cave he listens to Louis Armstrong.

Ellison does not reject those things that his narrator

rejects. Notice how sympathetically the black folk figures like Jim Trueblood and Mary Rambo are treated by Ellison. Why? What qualities do they have that Ellison seems to admire?

Note also the role of black music. There are a lot of "blues" in the novel, a form of music that expresses better than any other the essential nature of the black experience in America.

Test 2

1. B **2.** A **3.** B **4.** A **5.** B **6.** B
7. B **8.** B **9.** C **10.** B

11. Ellison, in his interview entitled "The Art of Fiction," talks about the symbolic use of the colors "black" and "white" to suggest not only the black and white races but also the traditional struggle between good and evil, so often symbolized in Western literature by black (evil) and white (good). You will see right away that there is a direct irony in the symbolism, because in a system of white racial superiority, whites pretend that they are good and blacks are evil, when it is often the reverse. Thus, Ellison's symbolism is very complicated, and it will require careful attention.

Look especially at Chapter 10 where Ellison uses the symbolism of black and white paint to play with the whole structure of American life. There is considerable commentary in this study guide on Chapter 10, where "Optic White Is the Right White" becomes the motto of a paint company whose real aim is to fool the public with optical illusions.

The symbolism of black and white is also associated with ignorance and knowledge, darkness and light. The narrator ends up in a black cave from which he will come up into the light at the end of the book. Is it the blackness of his skin or the ignorance of his mind that has led him into such darkness? Ellison invites *you* to explore such questions through his symbolism. He doesn't answer them easily.

12. This has been a particularly controversial subject, one that black critics and reviewers have disagreed widely about. You will find a range of opinions in the criticism and in the excerpts from The Critics.

You might approach this question by listing the major black characters in the novel and describing their behavior. Do they fall into certain groups and types? There are the southern educators, the Founder and Bledsoe; the black members of the Brotherhood, Brother Tarp and Tod Clifton; the black nationalist rabble-rouser, Ras the Exhorter; and the less-educated folk types—Jim Trueblood, Lucius Brockway, Mary Rambo, Peter Wheatstraw, and the unnamed yam seller. There is also the narrator himself, who seems to embody at one time or another, characteristics of all these types.

A quick look at these characters might indicate why some black radical writers thought Ellison was degrading blacks in his work. None of the characters is an ideal. They all have human flaws, some more so than others. Ellison certainly does not idealize his black characters, but he presents them as real human beings. Is he saying something about blacks in America by doing that?

On the other hand, Ellison does not treat all these groups alike. He seems considerably more sympathetic to characters like Tarp and Mary Rambo than he does toward Bledsoe, Ras, or Brother Wrestrum. You might analyze what Ellison seems particularly to like about the positive black characters before developing your thesis.

The section on The Characters will be particularly helpful to you, as will the commentaries in The Story section in the chapters where the particular characters are most important.

13. Here again, there is much room for debate. You may

find articles listed under Critical Works on both sides of the question. How can that be? Can a novel seem optimistic to some and pessimistic to others? This one can.

The optimists tend to look at the comedy in the novel, the word play, the humor, the obvious love for life that Ellison shows through the imagination and inventiveness of his style. They see the narrator as a comic hero, one who learns from his mistakes and comes out stronger for his experience. They see the novel as the story of a person who *does* finally find an identity and learn to be himself, and enjoy it. This is the story of the education of a young man, who will go on from the end of the novel to live a better and wiser life than the one he's experienced in this book. If you're an optimist, you will want to put some emphasis on the last couple of pages of the Epilogue where the narrator emphasizes such positive qualities as love and social responsibility.

The pessimists argue that the narrator undergoes a series of tragic adventures in which he is taken advantage of and abused over and over again. The world is so cruel to him that his only solution is to literally crawl into a black hole and hide. He ends up dropping out of the world because there is no place in it for him. Ellison's view of the world and the possibility of a place in it for a sensitive and thoughtful black man is pretty bleak. If there is hope at the end, it is a naive hope and one that is not really part of the action and its meaning. The emphasis for the pessimists is on the action and its meaning. For the optimists it is on the style and the tone.

14. *Invisible Man* may be read primarily as a story about the narrator's development. It is a first-person narrative, and because you experience the novel through the narrator, you get to know him better than anyone else. You must be careful, however, not to interpret the action the way he does, because that is to ignore his limitations and shortcomings as a character. Thus, to be able to interpret the action yourself, you must know where the narrator is in his development so that you can decide whether or not his judgment is reliable at that point in the novel.

One famous pattern of development is that of innocence to experience. At first the narrator is extremely innocent and does not understand what is happening to him. He does not believe people are bad. He does not see that Bledsoe is making a fool of him. As he suffers, he learns. With experience he begins to see the world more as it really is. Experience teaches him to be a better judge.

Whatever pattern you select, there is one certainty: The narrator *does change*. The questions are where? How? Why? And finally, how much? You might want especially to contrast the opening and closing chapters. The degree of change may determine your answer to the question of what sort of identity the narrator finally has.

15. A lot of blind and half-blind people and animals appear throughout *Invisible Man*. For starters, note that Brother Jack, the leader of the Brotherhood, has a glass eye. Note that throughout his first speech for the Brotherhood in Chapter 16 the narrator refers to black people as one-eyed mice. There is a direct allusion here to "Three Blind Mice." The idea is that black people start life with only one eye because of their racial situation, and that white people would just as soon have them lose the other eye in fighting one another. Then, you may remember, the whites blindfold the black boys during the battle royal in Chapter 1 so that they strike out blindly at each other.

These are just some blatant examples of Ellison's use of the imagery of sight and blindness in the novel. Sight, you may remember, is associated with *insight* or *perception* or *knowledge*. Blindness is associated with lack of these things, with *ignorance*, with *stupidity*. The imagery of sight and blindness is closely tied to the theme of invisibility. People are invisible because others do not see them. If you don't see someone, you are blind. Though the narrator can see physically, he is perceptually blind. So there is not always a direct association between physical blindness and figurative blindness. A fascinating example to study is the revelation at the end of Chapter 5 that Homer A. Barbee, the minister who has just told the story of the Founder so movingly, is blind. What might that mean?

Term Paper Ideas and other Topics for Writing

Themes

1. Discuss the theme of "invisibility."

2. Discuss the thematic use of "black" and "white" as colors, noting their symbolic uses both as racial and moral categories.

3. Examine the use of images of sight and blindness to develop the theme of perception or vision in the novel. Note particularly what characters see or do not see.

4. Explore *Invisible Man* as either a "black protest novel" or a "universal" novel. Which do you think was Ellison's primary intent? Why?

5. Discuss *Invisible Man* as a *bildungsroman*, the story of the education of a young man. Through what stages does the young man go? What does he learn?

Characters

1. Examine the protagonist as a "hero." What do you mean when you use the term "hero"? Is the narrator a hero to you?

2. Examine the major white characters—Mr. Norton, young Mr. Emerson, Brother Jack, and Kimbro in the paint factory. What does Ellison's portrayal of them suggest about his view of American whites?

3. Examine the Founder and Dr. Bledsoe as characters. What values do they represent? What is Ellison suggesting about those values?

4. What is Ellison's view of the Brotherhood? Examine closely the members of the Brotherhood, particularly the committee members (Jack, Tobitt, Wrestrum, Hambro). Why is Ellison critical of them?

5. Who is Rinehart? Look closely at him as both character and symbol. What is "Rinehartism"? What role does it play in the novel?

6. Discuss the symbolic role of Ras the Exhorter. What are his values, and to what extent is Ellison sympathetic toward or critical of them?

Influences, Sources, and Parallels

1. Ellison is often compared with Richard Wright. Read Wright's famous novel, *Native Son*, and compare it with *Invisible Man*. What are the similarities and differences?

2. *Invisible Man* is based partly on Richard Wright's long short story, "The Man Who Lived Underground." Read the story, and show how Ellison may have made use of it while writing *Invisible Man*.

3. A major inspiration for *Invisible Man* was Fyodor Dostoyevsky's *Notes from Underground*. Read that work and explore its influence on Ellison.

4. Many readers see parallels between *Invisible Man* and Joseph Conrad's *Heart of Darkness*. In what ways is that true?

5. One of Ralph Ellison's favorite poems was T. S. Eliot's *The Waste Land*. There are echoes of *The Waste Land* throughout *Invisible Man,* especially in the early chapters. Explore the parallels between the two works in an essay.

6. A major influence on Ellison was James Joyce. Discuss the parallels between Joyce's Stephen Dedalus (in *A Portrait of the Artist as a Young Man*) and the narrator of *Invisible Man*.

7. Ellison is frequently compared with the American black writer James Baldwin. Baldwin's book of essays, *Nobody Knows My Name*, is also concerned with the theme of invisibility. Discuss the parallels between Ellison and Baldwin.

8. Ralph Waldo Ellison was named after Ralph Waldo Emerson. Consider the influence of Emerson's ideas on *Invisible Man*. For additional background read ''Hidden Name and Complex Fate'' in Ellison's *Shadow and Act*.

The Reputation of *Invisible Man* and Ellison's Other Work

1. How good a novel is *Invisible Man*? It was highly praised when it first came out and won Ellison a prestigious National Book Award. Why do so many consider it to be one of the great American novels?

2. During the 1960s and early 70s many radical black leaders and writers denounced Ellison as being too easy on whites. Based on what you've learned about Ellison, was that criticism valid?

3. Writers on the political left denounced Ellison for his portrayal of the Brotherhood. Read an objective account of communism in America during the 1930s and 40s and see if you think Ellison was unfair.

4. *Invisible Man* is Ellison's only published novel. Read two or three of his short stories and compare them, thematically and stylistically, with the novel. Do you see characteristic themes and techniques in all of them?

5. Ellison's only other published book is *Shadow and Act*, a collection of essays and interviews. Read some of these and explore how the ideas might apply to *Invisible Man*.

Technique

1. Many consider Ellison a great stylist. How many different styles can you identify in the novel? Where does the style change and why?

2. Discuss Ellison's uses of folk materials, jazz, spirituals, and the traditional humor of blacks.

3. *Invisible Man* is written in the first person. Examine the novel as a first-person narrative, exploring what Ellison gains from the technique and what you must be aware of to get the most out of it.

4. Analyze the structure of the novel. Where are the major breaks and why?

5. Discuss Ellison's use of symbolic naming. You might include both characters and places. See the next section for specific suggestions.

Symbolism

Write an essay exploring one or more of the following objects, places, or events Ellison uses symbolically:

1. The "battle royal."

2. The iron bank in the narrator's room.

3. The Liberty Paint Factory.

4. Tod Clifton's dancing Sambo dolls.

5. The narrator's underground cellar or cave.

6. The Golden Day.

Write an essay exploring one or more of the following characters Ellison uses symbolically:

1. Jim Trueblood.

2. Mary Rambo.

3. Lucius Brockway.

Write an essay exploring Ellison's use of two of the following historical black figures in the novel:

1. Booker T. Washington.

2. Louis Armstrong.

3. Frederick Douglass.

4. Marcus Garvey.

Further Reading
CRITICAL WORKS

Baumbach, Jonathan. *The Landscape of Nightmare.* New York: New York University Press, 1965.

Bone, Robert. *Anger and Beyond.* New York: Harper & Row, 1966.

Gibson, Donald B., ed. *Five Black Writers.* New York: New York University Press, 1970.

Glicksberg, Charles I. "The Symbolism of Vision." *Southwest Review* 39 (Summer 1954), pp. 259–65.

Hersey, John, ed. *Ralph Ellison: A Collection of Critical Essays.* Englewood Cliffs, N.J.: Prentice-Hall, 1970.

Horowitz, Ellin. "The Rebirth of the Artist." In Richard Kostelanetz, ed. *On Contemporary Literature.* New York: Avon Books, 1964.

Horowitz, Floyd R. "Ralph Ellison's Modern Version of Brer Bear and Brer Rabbit in *Invisible Man*." *Midcontinent American Studies Journal* IV (2) (1963): 21–27.

Howe, Irving. *A World More Attractive*. New York: Horizon Press, 1963.

Kaiser, Ernest. "Negro Images in American Writing." *Freedomways* 7 (Spring 1967), pp. 152–63.

Klein, Marcus. *After Alienation*. Cleveland and New York: World Publishing Co., 1964.

Neal, Larry. "Ellison's Zoot Suit." *Black World* 20 (2) (December 1970), pp. 31–50.

Olderman, Raymond. "Ralph Ellison's Blues and *Invisible Man*." *Wisconsin Studies in Literature* 7 (1966): 142–57.

O'Meally, Robert G. *The Craft of Ralph Ellison*. Cambridge, Mass.: Harvard University Press, 1980.

———. "Ralph Ellison's Invisible Novel." *The New Republic* (January 17, 1981), pp. 26–29.

Reilly, John M., ed. *Twentieth Century Interpretations of Invisible Man*. Englewood Cliffs, N.J.: Prentice-Hall, 1970.

Rovit, Earl H. "Ralph Ellison and the American Comic Tradition." *Wisconsin Studies in Contemporary Literature* 1 (Fall 1960), pp. 34–42.

Schafer, William J. "Ralph Ellison and the Birth of the Anti-Hero." *Critique* 10 (1968): 81–93.

Tanner, Tony. In *City of Words: American Fiction, 1950–1970*. New York: Harper & Row, 1971.

Vogler, Thomas A. "*Invisible Man*: Somebody's Protest Novel." *Iowa Review* 1 (Spring 1970), pp. 64–82.

AUTHOR'S OTHER WORKS

Invisible Man is Ellison's first and only published novel. Since the publication of *Invisible Man* in 1952, Ellison has worked extensively on another novel, portions of which have been published as short stories. The long-awaited second novel had not appeared by the mid-1980s. Ellison's only other book-length work is *Shadow and Act* (New York: Random House, 1964), a collection of essays and interviews. Ellison's most important stories, essays, and interviews are listed below by title and date of original publication.

Stories

"Flying Home," In Edwin Seaver, ed. *Cross Section*. New York: L. B. Fischer, 1944, pp. 469–85.

"King of the Bingo Game," *Tomorrow* 3 (July 1944), pp. 29–33.

"And Hickman Arrives." *Noble Savage* 1 (1960): 5–49.

Essays

"Richard Wright's Blues." *Antioch Review*, 5 (Summer 1945), pp. 198–211.

"The World and the Jug," *New Leader* 46 (9 December 1963), pp. 22–26.

"Hidden Name and Complex Fate," In Ralph Ellison and Karl Shapiro, eds. *The Writer's Experience*. Washington, D.C.: Library of Congress, 1964, pp. 1–15.

"Remembering Jimmy," *Saturday Review* 41 (July 12, 1958), pp. 36–37.

"Introduction" to *Invisible Man*. Thirtieth Anniversary Edition. New York: Vintage Books, 1982.

Inteviews

"The Art of Fiction: An Inteview," *Paris Review* 8 (Spring 1955), pp. 55–71.

"That Same Pain, That Same Pleasure: An Interview." R. G. Stern. *December* 3 (Winter 1961), pp. 30–32, 37–46.

"Introduction: A Completion of Personality" (interview with John Hersey). In John Hersey, ed. *Ralph Ellison: A Collection of Critical Essays*. Englewood Cliffs, N.J.: Prentice-Hall, 1974.

The Critics

Central Themes

Well, there are certain themes, symbols and images which are based on folk material. For example, there is the old saying amongst Negroes: If you're black, stay back; if you're brown, stick around; if you're white, you're right. And there is the joke Negroes tell on themselves about their being so black they can't be seen in the dark. In my book this sort of thing was merged with the meanings which blackness and light have long had in Western mythology: evil and goodness, ignorance and knowledge, and so on. In my novel the narrator's development is one through blackness to light; that is, from ignorance to enlightenment: invisibility to visibility. He leaves the South and goes North; this, as you will notice in reading Negro folktales, is always the road to freedom—the movement upward. You have the same thing again when he leaves his underground cave for the open.

—Ralph Ellison, "The Art of Fiction:
An Interview," 1955

The Symbolism of Vision

Ralph Ellison, in *Invisible Man*, relies heavily on the symbolism of vision: light, color, perception, sight, insight. These, his master symbols, are organically related to the dualism of black and white, the all-absorbing and bafflingly complex problem of identity. How does the Negro see himself and how do others see him? Do they notice him at all? Do they really see him as he is or do they behold a stereotype, a ghostly caricature, a traditionally accepted myth? What we get in this novel, creatively elaborated, is the drama of symbolic action, the language of the eyes, the incredibly complex and subtle symbolism of vision. All this is structurally bound up with the underlying theme of transformation. All this is imaginatively and, for the most part, successfully worked out in terms of fiction.

—Charles I. Glicksberg, "The
Symbolism of Vision," 1954

The Narrator as Artist

A profitable method of dealing with *Invisible Man* is to see the action as a series of initiations in which the hero passes through several stages and groups of identification. The changes of identity are accompanied by somewhat formal rituals resembling the primitive's rites of passage. The primitive recognizes that man changes his identity as he passes from one stage or group to another and accompanies this transition by rituals that are essentially symbolic representations of birth, purification and regeneration in nature.

Ellison's narrative is a series of such initiatory experiences set within a cyclical framework of the mystic initiation of the artist. The rites of passage take the hero through several stages in which he acts out his various and conflicting sub-personalities. When he has won his freedom he is reborn as the artist, the only actor in our society whose "end" is a search beneath the label for what is individual.

—*Ellin Horowitz, "The Rebirth of the Artist," 1964*

Ellison's Depiction of the Communists

If *Native Son* is marred by the ideological delusions of the thirties, *Invisible Man* is marred, less grossly, by those of the fifties. The middle section of Ellison's novel, dealing with the Harlem Communists, does not ring quite true, in the way a good portion of the writings on this theme during the post-war years does not ring quite true. Ellison makes his Stalinist figures so vicious and stupid that one cannot understand how they could ever have attracted him or any other Negro. That the party leadership manipulated members with deliberate cynicism is beyond doubt, but this cynicism was surely more complex and guarded than Ellison shows it to be. No party leader would ever tell a prominent Negro Communist, as one of them does in *Invisible Man:* "You were not hired [as a functionary] to think"— even if that were what he felt. Such passages are almost as damaging as the propagandist outbursts in *Native Son*.

—*Irving Howe*, A World More
Attractive, 1963

The Protagonist as Universal Man

I hesitate to call Ralph Ellison's *Invisible Man* (1952) a Negro novel, though of course it is written by a Negro and is centrally concerned with the experiences of a Negro. The appellation is not so much inaccurate as it is misleading. A novelist treating the invisibility and phantasmagoria of the Negro's life in this "democracy" is, if he tells the truth, necessarily writing a very special kind of book. Yet if his novel is interesting only because of its specialness, he has not violated the surface of his subject; he has not, after all, been serious. Despite the differences in their external concerns, Ellison has more in common as a novelist with Joyce, Melville, Camus, Kafka, West, and Faulkner than he does with other serious Negro writers like James Baldwin and Richard Wright. To concentrate on the idiom of a serious novel, no matter how distinctive its peculiarities, is to depreciate it, to minimize the universality of its implications. Though the protagonist of *Invisible Man* is a southern Negro, he is, in Ellison's rendering, profoundly all of us.

—*Jonathan Baumbach*, The
Landscape of Nightmare, 1965

The Design of the Plot

The plot structure of *Invisible Man* is schematic. The novel uses a cumulative plot (in M. C. Bradbrook's illuminating terminology), developing the same basic episode over and over in an emotional crescendo: the protagonist struggles idealistically to live by the commandments of his immediate social group, then is undone by the hypocrisy built into the social structure and is plunged into despair. This happens in four large movements: 1) the struggle into college, the failure with Norton and expulsion from the "paradise" of the college; 2) job-hunting in New York, Emerson's disillusioning lecture and the battle and explosion at Liberty Paints; 3) the "resurrection" or reconstruction of the protagonist, his plunge into radical activism and his purge by the Brotherhood; 4) the meeting with Rinehart, the beginning of the riots and the protagonist's confrontation and defeat of Ras, ending in the flight underground. Each episode is a development to a climax followed by a peripeteia. The novel's prologue and epilogue simply frame this series of climaxes and reversals and interpret the emotional collapse of the invisible man in the present tense.

—*William J. Schafer, "Ralph Ellison and the Birth of the Anti-Hero,"* 1968

The Symbolism of Names

Characters' names, and the club names, and the names of factories, places and institutions—even the names of things, like the Sambo doll—can be explored indefinitely in this novel. The Brotherhood has its parties at a place called the Chthonian Club, which is a classical reference comparable to that of the Sybils. The Chthonian realm belonged to the underground gods and spirits; and true power for Ellison is an underground influence as we learn from seeing Bledsoe and Brockway and Brother Jack in action, as well as the invisible man writing in his hole. Where does Ras get his name, with its vocal nearness to "race"? He gives it to himself, as the invisible man gives us the name we must call him by if we are to know him for what he is.

—*Thomas A. Vogler, "Invisible Man: Somebody's Protest Novel,"* 1970

The Narrator's Odyssey to Selfhood

The odyssey which the narrator, with the aid of 1,369 light bulbs, looks back on takes place on many levels. His travelling is geographic, social, historical and philosophical. In an early dream he finds inside his brief-case an envelope which contains an endless recession of smaller envelopes, the last of which contains the simple message "Keep This Nigger-Boy Running." It is only at the end when he finally burns all the contents of his real brief-case that he can start to control his own momentum. Up to that point his movements are really controlled from without, just like the people in the New York streets who to him seem to walk as though they were directed by "some unseen control." The pattern of his life is one of constraint and eviction; he is alternately cramped and dispossessed. This is true of his experience in the college, the factory, the hospital, the Party. What he discovers is that every institution is bent on processing and programming the individual in a certain way; yet if a man does not have a place in any of the social structures the danger is that he might fall into chaos.

—*Tony Tanner, "The Music of Invisibility,"* 1973 ⟩

The Wisdom of Black Folk Experience

Invisible Man is not a historical novel, of course, but it deals with the past as a burden and as a stepping stone to the future. The hero discovers that history moves not like an arrow or an objective, scientific argument, but like a boomerang: swiftly, cyclically, and dangerously. He sees that when he is not conscious of the past, he is liable to be slammed in the head with it again when it circles back. As the novel unfolds, the Invisible Man learns that by accepting and evaluating all parts of his experience, smooth and ragged, loved and unloved, he is able to "look around corners" into the future:

At the beginning of the novel, the Invisible Man presents himself as a kind of Afro-American Jonathan, a "green" yokel pushed into the clownhouse of American society. He starts out ignorant of his society, his past, himself. By the end of the book he accepts his southern black folk past and sees that ordinary blacks like his grandfather, Trueblood, Mary, Tarp, Dupre, the unnamed boys in the subway, and himself are of ultimate value, no matter what the Bledsoes and Jacks say. Jarred to consciousness by folklore (among other things), the Invisible Man realizes that the tested wisdom expressed in spirituals, blues, dozens, and stories is a vital part of his experience. At last he comprehends that whatever he might do to be "so black and blue," he is, simply, who he is.

—*Robert G. O'Meally*, The Craft of
Ralph Ellison, 1980